L. C. Probyn

Indian Coinage And Currency

L. C. Probyn

Indian Coinage And Currency

ISBN/EAN: 9783741103605

Manufactured in Europe, USA, Canada, Australia, Japa

Cover: Foto ©Lupo / pixelio.de

Manufactured and distributed by brebook publishing software
(www.brebook.com)

L. C. Probyn

Indian Coinage And Currency

INDIAN COINAGE AND CURRENCY

ABERDEEN UNIVERSITY PRESS.

AND

CURRENCY

PAPERS ON AN INDIAN GOLD STANDARD, WITH
THE INDIAN COINAGE AND CURRENCY
ACTS CORRECTED TO DATE

BY

L. C. PROBYN

LONDON
EFFINGHAM WILSON
11 ROYAL EXCHANGE, E.C.
1897

PREFACE.

THE interest which is now being taken in the possible re-opening of the Indian Mints to the coinage of silver as part of a bimetallic agreement with the United States and France induces me to publish in a collected form several papers on the subject of Indian money. They are reprinted as they were written, added remarks being shown as footnotes between brackets, thus : [   ].

Much of what was written has been justified by subsequent events. The closure of the Mints to the coinage of silver in June, 1893, avowed by the Government as the first step towards the attainment of a gold standard, justifies the advice for the adoption of that measure with that object five years earlier. The system of a rupee rate for the receipt of gold, and of making the currency reserve the medium of exchanging such gold into silver, which was adopted by executive order in 1893, was suggested, but as a legal obligation, in 1888 and 1892. The suggestion in 1892 of 1s. 3d., an approximation to its gold value at the time, as the permanent value for the rupee, has been proved to have been sound, not merely by its failure to rise to 1s. 4d., the limit temporarily adopted when the Mints were closed, but also by the success which is apparently attending the Russian and Japanese standard conversions at about the ratio of the day.   •

There has been yet no opportunity for proving the correctness of my contention that, in a country circumstanced as India is, where the bulk of the transactions are too small for the convenient use of gold, and where a large paper currency exists under the control of the State, Ricardo's plan, advocated for India by Lord Sherbrooke, for a paper currency convertible into uncoined gold, could be conveniently extended to the conversion of silver coins into uncoined gold, so as to put the whole silver rupee currency on an effective gold basis. But none of my critics have shown the plan to be theoretically unsound or practically impossible.

It will be seen that the proposals to amend the Indian Coinage and Paper Currency Acts have been embodied in the form of a Draft Bill. Doubtless many imperfections can be discovered in it. But the desire to make my scheme absolutely clear overcame the scruples which I otherwise would have had in submitting it in this form.

In this connection, and also because there is much ignorance, even among those who should be better informed, of the actual state of the law, the Indian Coinage and Currency Acts as they stand amended to date, together with the Notifications of 26th June, 1893, have been printed. It is believed the only other Acts in force affecting the currency are the Native States Coinage Act IX., of 1876, which empowers under certain conditions the coinage for Native States of rupees identical with Government rupees, but which has only been adopted by two States, and the Bhopal Coinage Act XI., of 1897, a temporary Act to permit the Currency Department advancing part of its reserves while Bhopal were being re-coined into Government rupees.

A diagram, suggested by an article in the *Times* of the 18th of August last, showing the variations in the gold value of silver and of the coined rupee since 1892, has been added. It demonstrates conclusively the error of those who held that on the closure of the Mints silver would in its fall drag down the rupee with it.

A chronology of some of the principal events affecting the question has also been added for facility of reference.

As this book is passing through the press the India Council, while altogether suspending for ten weeks the sale of bills on India, has commenced to buy them. It sold nearly ten lakhs on the 1st of September at 1s. $3\frac{13}{16}$d., and bought a crore six days later at 1s. $4\frac{1}{16}$d. ! The financial necessities which led to this step must have been very grave. The forced rise in exchange already caused by the limited sale of bills (eight crores less having been sold since the 1st of April last than in the corresponding period of 1896) was intensified by this measure, and it is feared that the reaction which followed the forced rise in exchange in the latter half of 1893 must again result. If the position in India was so serious, and if it could not have been met by a loan in that country, then gold should have been purchased either in London or Australia for the Indian currency reserves, a corresponding amount in rupees being freed, the State thus doing what would have been done by private individuals if the suggestions I made in 1892 had been adopted. An unsatisfactory feature in the present situation, connected no doubt with the forced rise in exchange and the uncertainty as to the future of the rupee, is the decline in the amount of rupee paper on the London books; this is four crores less than at the beginning of the year. The necessity for a currency which shall act automatically is emphasised by what is occurring.

L. C. PROBYN.

13th September, 1897.

CONTENTS.

Diagram shewing the relative value of the Rupee, and of Silver, in gold.

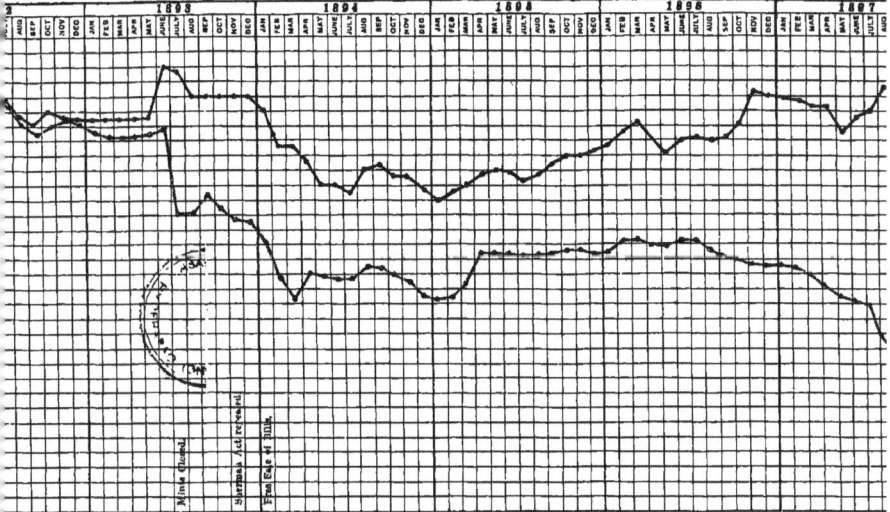

The average exchange value of the Rupee realised by the Indian Government was in

1893-4	14.547 pence.	
1894-5	13.101 "	
1895-6	13.680 "	
1896-7	14.449 "	

Rupee Maximum, June 27, 1893, 16$\frac{1}{32}$d.

Rupee Minimum, Jan. 28, 1895, 12$\frac{19}{32}$d.

Silver Minimum, Aug. 26, 1897, 29$\frac{3}{4}$d.

The values are taken at the mean price between the highest and the lowest in each month.

Index Numbers in the Diagram are arranged to show the approximate melting value of the Rupee alongside of each Price of er. As the Rupee contains $\frac{45}{148}$ of the Pure Silver contained in an Ounce of (so called) Standard Silver, the progression of $\frac{3}{4}$d. in the Rupee column practically corresponds to that of 1d. in the Silver column.

Diagram shewing the relative value of the Rupee, and of Silver, in gold.

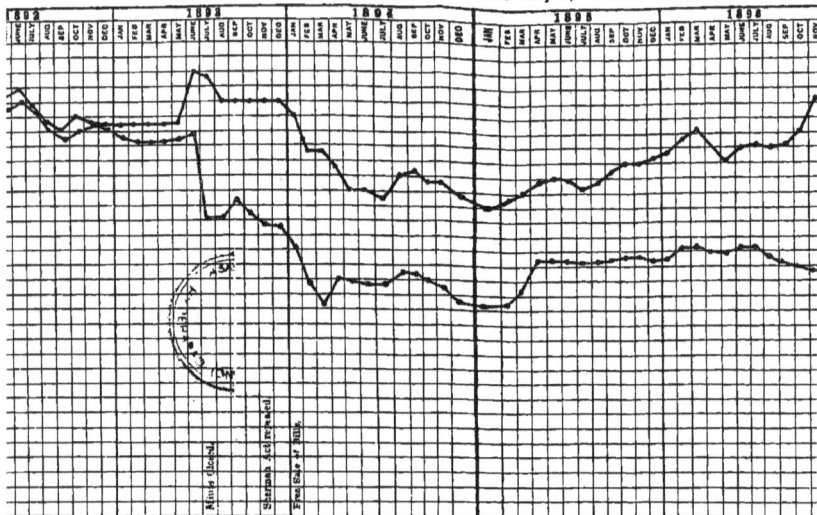

The average exchange value of the Rupee realised by the Indian Government was in

1893-4   14.547 pence.   Rupee Maximum, June 27, 1893, :
1894-5   13.101   ,,   Rupee Minimum, Jan. 28, 1895, :
1895-6   13.690   ,,
1896-7   14.449   ,,   Silver Minimum, Aug. 26, 1897, :

The values are taken at the mean price between the highest and

The Index Numbers in the Diagram are arranged to show the approximate melting value of the Rupee alongside Silver. As the Rupee contains 45/48 of the Pure Silver contained in an Ounce of (so called) Standard Silver, the p in the Rupee column practically corresponds to that of 1d. in the Silver column.

IMPORTANT EVENTS CONNECTED WITH INDIAN CURRENCY ARRANGED IN CHRONOLOGICAL ORDER.

1835. Silver established as the standard of value of British India.

1861. Indian Government paper currency system established with fiduciary issue of Rx. 6,000,000. Fiduciary issue raised in 1890 to Rx. 8,000,000, and in 1896 to Rx. 10,000,000.

1874. *January.* Limitage of coinage of full legal tender silver by the States of the Latin Union.

1878. *January.* Passage of "Bland Act" in United States of America compelling the purchase by the Treasury for coinage into dollars of not less than 2,000,000 dollars worth of silver every month.

1878. *November.* Suspension of coinage of full legal tender silver by the States of the Latin Union.

1890. *July.* Passage of "Sherman Act" in United States of America repealing the "Bland Act" of 1878, and compelling the purchase by the Treasury each month of 4,500,000 ounces of silver bullion.

1893. *June.* Closure of the Indian Mints to the coinage of silver for the public.

1893. *November.* Repeal of the "Sherman Act" in the United States of America.

A PROPOSED GOLD STANDARD FOR INDIA
(1888).

(A paper read before the East India Association on 11th June, 1888.)

THE maxim " *quieta non movere* " has peculiar force in questions connected with coinage and currency, and to justify departure from its injunctions in such matters it is necessary to show the existence of serious evils. Before, therefore, explaining my proposal for introducing a gold standard into India, I will briefly point out the injuries which, as it appears to me, are being caused to that country by her present monetary system. I believe I could show that these injuries re-act with great force on England, and that the remedy which I am about to suggest is not inconsistent with the direct interests of this country ; but I propose in this paper to look at the question from an Indian point of view alone.

1. The trade between India and gold standard countries is injuriously affected by the variations in the relative values of silver and gold. These variations it is impossible for the most acute trader to foresee. They are dependent, not only on the ordinary laws which govern production—and these are peculiarly unstable in the case of the precious metals—but on the actions of Governments which it is impossible to anticipate. The first ·cause of the serious fluctuations which have occurred was, as is well known, the adoption of a gold standard in Germany ; and

1

even now the action of the United States Congress is looked forward to with anxiety from day to day; and if its action, or that of the French Government, resulted in throwing large stocks of silver on the market, we might have even greater changes in the future than we have had in the past. As to the effect on trade of such variations, I will quote two very high authorities. Mr. Goschen, speaking in Parliament on the 12th of June, 1879, said that the violent fluctuations of the exchange of late years had been disastrous to many, and a great trial to the whole Indian trade. Sir Louis Mallet, at the monetary conference in Paris in 1881, said: "In my opinion then trade sustains an evil and a very serious one". On this subject much evidence of value has been given before the Gold and Silver Commission; and, though it appeared that the injury to trade had more directly affected England than India, it is manifest that in the long run the trade of the one country cannot suffer without detriment to that of the other. I know it has been the custom to talk as if the Indian export trade had received a permanent stimulus from cheap silver. But that such is not the opinion of one very well qualified to judge will be seen from the evidence of Mr. H. Waterfield, Financial Secretary at the India Office, who said (Answer 2499): "I can see no evidence that the increase which has taken place (in the Indian exports) is due to the fall in exchange".

2. The flow of capital from gold standard countries to India is stopped by the uncertainty which prevails as to the value of silver. In theory, of course, the return on invested capital ought not to be dependent on exchange. But, practically, people are afraid of investing in a country, the standard of which is constantly depreciating with reference to their own. There is urgent need for the in-

vestment of fresh capital in India. Railways are wanted
for its development. Its manufacturing power is capable
°of almost indefinite expansion. Its mineral resources are
believed to be vast. Its internal trade is open to immense
extension. One witness examined before the Gold and
Silver Commission (Answer 2882), thinks " that from
£15,000,000 to £20,000,000 might be earned as an annual
dividend on money in England for investments in silver-
using countries, if the money could be protected from the
effects of this uncertainty ". He was speaking of the injury that British capitalists suffered. It is no less evidence of the injury which India suffers from the loss of
capital. A striking instance of the difficulty with which
money flows to India will be found in the comparison of
the rates of discount in India and England at the same
time. It sometimes happens that high rates of discount
prevail for considerable periods in India, while low rates
are prevalent in Europe.

3. The credit of the Indian Government in its own
standard currency is seriously affected by its unsatisfactory character. In 1873, 4 per cent. rupee loans in
India stood at 105. They now stand at a trifle over par.
In 1873, 4 per cent. sterling stock stood at 106. The $3\frac{1}{2}$
per cent. sterling stock is now slightly above that figure.
Thus while the credit of the Indian Government (measured by the rate at which it can borrow money) in its
own standard has fallen more than 4 per cent., in gold it
has risen $12\frac{1}{2}$ per cent. A further illustration of the
difference between the credit of the Indian Government
in silver and in gold will be found in the following fact.
Taking the present exchange as the rate at which rupee
interest drafts can be sold, an investor can, even after
allowing for the Indian Income Tax to which this class of
investment is liable, obtain £4 per cent. for his money by

investing in rupee securities, against only £3 6s. per cent. from investments in sterling.*

It should be borne in mind that rupee and sterling • loans are alike guaranteed by the Government of India alone. The security for payment of interest and principal, there being no Imperial guarantee, is identical in both cases. The only difference is the description of money which is borrowed. It is, in fact, the insecurity of the monetary standard itself which depreciates the value of the silver investment. As the 4½ per cent. rupee loans are repayable in 1893, and the 4 per cent. loans at three months' notice, it is not too much to say that a present annual loss of £500,000 is caused to the Indian tax-payer by this insecurity of the standard, to say nothing of the prospective injury in the event of further borrowings in silver.

4. Then there is the question of what is known as *the loss by exchange;* that is, the additional sum which the Indian Government has to pay in its standard currency to meet its obligations in gold. Writing in 1879, the Indian Government said: " The current of all the most trust-worthy opinion tends more and more towards the conclu-sion that so far as can now be foreseen there is no prospect of any early or complete recovery in the value of silver, and, on the contrary, that the probabilities are all in favour of a further fall ". Notwithstanding the doubt thrown on this opinion by the Lords Commissioners of H.M.'s Treasury, events have justified it ; the loss by exchange in 1886-7 having been about Rx. 2,000,000 more than in 1880-81. Roughly speaking, it may be said that a fall of 1d. in the exchange, which would result from a fall of about 3d. per

---

* [The difference resulting from investing in rupee and sterling secu-rities of the Government of India has rather lessened since the closure of the mints.]

ounce in the price of bar silver, means a loss to the Indian
Government of about Rx. 1,000,000.   The total excess loss
• by exchange between the 1st April, 1875, and 31st March,
1888, over what it would have been had the exchange
remained at what it was in 1874-75, amounts to no less
a sum than Rx. 29,277,632.   It is sometimes forgotten
what a great injury this is to the Indian tax-payer, an
injury for which he is not sufficiently compensated by the
silver that he is accumulating in hoards and ornaments.

5. For the people of India are suffering a serious and
increasing loss by receiving and hoarding a metal which
they are taking in ignorance of its falling value in the
markets of the world.*   Its value in India is kept up
fictitiously by its being coined by the Government, by its
being still recognised as the standard of the country, and
by its being used for ornaments and hoarding.   But its
value in the world generally has fallen, and is still falling.
It is the duty of a Government to look after the interests
of its subjects.   Is the British Government of India doing
this in encouraging the acceptance by the people of a
commodity, the value of which is only maintained by such
acceptance?   The East India Association was instituted
for the promotion of the welfare of the inhabitants of
India.   Is it, I ask, for their welfare that hundreds of

* Between 1st April, 1874, and 31st March, 1887, the net imports of
silver into India amounted to Rx. 89,077,000. The gold value of this, calculated on the average price of silver each year, was £71,049,000. The
present value, taken at 42½d. per ounce, is £58,103,000. There has thus
been a loss of £12,946,000 on the gold value of silver imported into India
during these thirteen years, a loss of a million a year to the people of
India.

[Carrying the figures down to 31st March, 1893, and taking silver at
even 30d. an ounce (and it has touched 23¾d.), there is a difference of about
£43,000,000 between the gold value of silver at date of import and its
present gold value. In other words, if India had imported gold instead
of silver between April, 1874, and March, 1893, she would have been
£43,000,000 richer than she is.]

tons of unfructifying silver should every year find their
way into the homes of the people ? Sooner or later the
true value of silver in the markets of the world must •
assert itself in India. Sooner or later the people must
find out the mistake they have made in hoarding it. The
longer the evil day is postponed the more serious will be
the consequences of the discovery.

6. The question of the home remittances and pensions
of Indian officers has often been referred to as one of the
manifest evils of the depreciated standard. No doubt it
has caused serious loss to the officers affected, but the
evil appears to me smaller than any of the others to which
I have drawn attention. And what perhaps makes it of
less importance is the loyalty of our Indian services of all
classes, who have submitted to this loss, and will continue
to submit to it, not perhaps without a murmur, but
certainly without deviating from their duty to the Government and country they so loyally serve.

To understand the remedy which I propose, it is
necessary that the difference between the monetary *standard* and the *currency* of a country should be thoroughly
appreciated. The two terms are sometimes used indis-
criminately, because the *standard* and *currency* often,
though of course not necessarily, go together. Thus, in
England our standard is gold ; and the gold sovereign and
the gold half-sovereign, which (when of full weight) are
standard coins, form a material part of the money in
current circulation. They are, therefore, alike *standard*
and *current* coins. On the other hand (although we often
talk of "standard silver"), the silver and copper coins
current in England are not standard money at all. It is
the custom to call silver and copper coins circulating as
current money in a gold standard country "tokens".
Tokens may be defined as pieces of metal, or, as Mr.

Goschen once called them, "*metallic notes*," which the issuer undertakes to accept at their nominal value, and to
redeem if presented in sufficient quantities. They are in point of fact (although in this matter our English coinage law does not, as I think unfortunately, bear out our English practice) *promises to pay.* To understand my proposal this point must be borne in mind. A shilling, for instance, is current money, not because of its intrinsic value, which indeed is only about $\frac{1}{30}$* of £1, but because it is a promise to pay $\frac{1}{20}$ of £1. It is obligatory on every one to take it as the twentieth part of a sovereign in all small transactions, and practically any one can exchange twenty of these "promissory medals" for a sovereign.

For two reasons these *promises to pay* are made on metal instead of on paper.

1. Metal coins are more convenient for carrying about, and for passing from hand to hand for small ordinary every-day transactions, than pieces of paper which can be less easily handled and which need constant renewal.

2. Paper *promises to pay* are more liable to forgery than metallic tokens. In a country with a well-ordered gold standard, silver tokens have an intrinsic value nearly, though not quite, reaching the nominal value of the gold they represent. Their forgery, if made of baser metal than they purport to be made of, can be readily detected. If they were made of good metal, to yield any profit (the difference between the real and nominal value being small) they would have to be made on a large scale, and the danger of detection would be great.

It is most important to guard against the over-issue of a token currency. The simplest and most effectual safe-

* [Now, with silver at 25d., less than $\frac{1}{13}$ of £1.]

guard is for the issuing authority to be in a position, and to undertake, when called on, to redeem any portion of the token currency in full standard money. If this be done there can be no danger of over-issue ; and, except for the considerations of convenience and safety above explained, with this precaution a token currency may as well be of paper as of metal.

But if this precaution be not adopted there will be a danger of over-issue. The currency will not be susceptible of automatic contraction, and the greater the proportion of the token currency to the standard currency of the country, the greater will be the danger of this automatic contraction not taking effect. Should circumstances be such that the tokens issued amount to more than the requirements of the country, and they cannot be changed into full standard money, they will fall to a discount, just in the same way as is the case in a country with an inconvertible paper currency. But at the same time it is possible so to manage the token currency of a country that, even without the guarantee of being able to exchange into full standard money, over-issue can be guarded against. The silver five-franc piece in France, the dollar in America, is each a mere token—in neither case is it full standard money.*   In neither country can it be changed into gold. Yet through the action of the Bank of France in the one case, and of the Treasury in the other, these silver tokens are sustained at par, and are effectual for the internal transactions of the country.

Having thus cleared the way by explaining the nature of current coins which are not standard money, I will now,

---

* [In the discussion which followed the reading of this paper Mr. H. Schmidt objected to this description of a token, arguing, as I think, without justification, that the real distinctive characteristic of a token is its *limited* legal tender property.]

by way of illustration, and to make my proposal clearer,
state a purely hypothetical case, taken from the standard
and currency of England. Under our British Coinage
Act, provision is made for the coinage of 10s., £1, £2, and
£5 gold-pieces. Supposing an Act were passed discon-
tinuing the coinage of sovereigns and half-sovereigns, and
merely leaving the £2 and £5 gold-pieces, what effect
would this have on our standard of value? Ignorant
people might say at first that we had altered our standard.
There would be many complaints against the change,
which would be a great practical innovation, and one to
which there would be many valid objections. But if provision were made requiring the Mint or some other insti-
tution to give to all-comers silver in exchange for £2
pieces, and £2 pieces in exchange for silver, there would
be no difference whatever, either in our home standard of
value or in our foreign exchanges. As the sovereigns and
half-sovereigns gradually disappeared from circulation,
there would be a demand for additional silver coins to take
their places. Unless some provision were made for the
issue of small paper notes, we should have to carry about
an inconvenient amount of silver, and our every-day
transactions would not be carried on so easily as they are
at present. There would be other objections which need
not at present be discussed. But there would be no
alteration whatever in the standard, although there might
not be one single sovereign left in circulation. I will
take my illustration one step further. Supposing that
the Legislature likewise stopped the coinage of the £2
and £5 gold-pieces, and authorised bars of gold exactly
ten times the size of the £5 gold-piece to be made and
stamped, and to be legal tender for £50; supposing that
the necessary alterations were made in the Bank Act, so
as to make it lawful for the Bank to pay notes, except

when brought in parcels of £50 and upwards, in silver tokens; supposing that the legal tender limit of silver tokens were raised from 40s. (as it is at present) to £5 ; • there would still be no alteration in the standard, though there might be grave practical objections to this proposal.

One step further. Let me raise the bar of gold from £50 to £7500, and alter the limit of the obligation of the bank to pay its notes in gold in the same way. Our £5 bank-notes would be as good as they ever were.* The gold to secure them would be in the bank just as much as it is at present. But no one would be entitled to demand it unless he brought £7500 worth of bank-notes. Practically, of course, much of the work now done by gold sovereigns would be done by silver, or by paper. In the case of the former there would be direct economy of gold. In the case of the latter there would be no economy, except the saving of the loss by abrasion, unless either a larger investment of the Reserve were authorised, or a larger part of it came to be held in silver.

The practical objections which could be advanced against such a scheme for England might be insuperable, but the standard, it will be seen, would remain exactly as it is at present.

This, however, is the scheme which I propose for India. It would result in her having precisely the same standard as England, and the alteration would, I believe, be introduced with a minimum of change in the existing currency arrangements of the country.

I propose that gold bars each containing 40 lbs. 1 oz.

* [Mr. Hermann Schmidt in the discussion which followed the reading of the paper questioned this conclusion, arguing that the notes would soon fall practically to a discount. I do not agree with him. On the contrary I believe it would prevent the premium on bar gold which sometimes exists at present.]

10 dwts. 20 grains of gold eleven-twelfths fine, and corresponding, therefore, exactly to 1875 sovereigns, should be
made, and that four, representing in value £7500, should
be legal tender for 100,000 or one lakh of rupees.* (I
have suggested four bars, weighing only about 40 lbs.
each, as more convenient for handling than one bar of
160 lbs.) I propose that four of these bars linked together should be the basis of the Indian standard of value
just as the sovereign is at present the basis of the British
standard.

I propose that any one who brings sufficient gold for
the purpose should be entitled to have it made, subject to
a small charge to cover the cost of melting and refining,
into four of these bars, or that he should receive, in exchange for his gold, a note for Rs. 100,000, payable at the
option of the holder either in silver rupees or gold bars.
I propose, further, that the currency offices and all the
treasuries in India should be allowed, under suitable
arrangements with the assay offices, to receive gold in
quantities of two ounces and upwards, giving in exchange,
subject to a small charge to cover the cost of melting and
refining, silver rupees and currency notes at the rate of
one rupee for every 8·475 grains of pure gold, or, in other
words, one rupee for 1s. 6d.

The Indian mints would be closed for all coinage
except on Government account, but the public by bringing
gold could put the Government in motion, and the total
amount coined would thus depend on the wants and
action of the public. Government rupees and currency

* [I believe now that the suggested gold unit was unnecessarily high ;
later on I modified my views, suggesting a gold unit of Rs. 10,000 only.
See page 41. Perhaps also it would be needlessly confusing to declare
the bars themselves legal tender, and this was accordingly omitted in my
subsequent paper. The notes representing the bars would of course be
legal tender.]

notes secured on them as at present would continue to be full legal tender and the ordinary current money of the country.

It is true they would not be full standard money. The rupee would only be a token of $\frac{1}{100000}$th part of four quarter-lakh gold bars; and for some time no doubt it would not be possible to secure the exchange of Rs. 100,000 into their gold equivalent. The only full standard money would be the gold bars and the one-lakh notes. Gradually, as the currency reserve came to be held in gold, the currency notes, being based more and more on gold and less and less on silver, would approach the conditions of full standard money. Meanwhile, the currency notes, other than the one-lakh notes, would be promises to pay in rupees, and the rupees themselves would be only tokens.*

I have taken the rate at 18d.† per rupee. There is no special virtue in this particular, or indeed any even, number of pence. But it is sufficiently near the present price to avoid any great change in value. The rate should not be taken too high. The closure of the Indian mints against the general coinage of silver will have the effect of reducing still further the gold price of that metal. Unless, therefore, some great and unexpected change should take place, the intrinsic value of the rupee will be considerably less than 18d., and any higher figure would increase the divergence between the intrinsic and nominal or standard value of the token, and so increase the risk of its illicit fabrication. And there is another point worth consideration. The measure of the value of all com-

---

* [Imperfect tokens: see below, page 33.]

† [When this paper was read the rupee was worth about 16d. Subsequent consideration showed the inexpediency of attempting any material increase in its gold value as a monopoly coin. Accordingly four and a half years later I only proposed to raise it from 14⅜d. to 15d. See page 40.]

modities in the country will be the new standard.
Government rupees will have their token value. But
• all other silver, including the vast amount of ornaments
of that metal in the country, and the great quantity of
silver doubtless hoarded in other forms than Government
rupees, will be measured by the new standard. A tolah
of silver instead of being worth one rupee, as at present,
will be worth, if silver falls to 40d. an ounce, only 13
annas 2¼ pies of the new money.

The apparent fall of even 17½ per cent. in the value of
their hoards would no doubt be considered a hardship to
the owners, and indeed it has been suggested to me might
be a cause of serious discontent. It is well, therefore,
not to fix the gold value of the rupee too high. If it were
taken at say two shillings, the tolah of silver would be
worth less than 10 annas.

I have specified the four bars of gold which are to be
the basis of the Indian standard at a very large figure.
There is of course no particular virtue in the exact weight
of gold suggested; but a lakh of rupees is a good round
sum, thoroughly understood. My object is, by placing
the value of the pieces of gold legalised as currency as
high as possible, to discourage the use of that metal for
the purpose. Not only by this method is there more
employment found for the large number of silver rupees
already in existence, but there is also economy of gold,
and there would not be the temptation to hoard which
would be encouraged if gold coins were to be put in circulation.

There is an important difference between the system
proposed for India and that described in my illustration,
which will not escape notice. In my illustration, the
Bank of England was liable to give gold in exchange for
silver and parcels of notes of not less value than the legal

tender bar of gold. In my proposal for India, this liability
has been omitted. The rupees and the currency notes,
other than the one-lakh notes, will be better tokens than
the five-franc pieces of the Latin Union and the Bland
dollars of the United States, for the intrinsic value of the
silver rupee will much more nearly approach its nominal
gold value than will be the case with the French and
American silver coins. But bearing in mind the definition
I have given, they will not be perfect tokens. Arrangements are not made for their redemption if presented in
sufficient quantities, and provision is not, therefore, made
for the automatic contraction of the currency. It happens,
however, that, in the case of India, the imperfection of a
non-contracting currency is of comparatively small importance.

The accompanying statement * of the net import of
the precious metals into India for the last fourteen years
shows that even after allowing for the large payments
which have to be made in England, on account of the
Government, there is still a large balance of indebtedness
which has to be adjusted by bullion remittances. In this
table no account is taken of money borrowed in England,
but even after allowing for these amounts there is still a
large balance at the credit of India, and this has been the
case for fifty years. Not only, therefore, will none of her
standard be abstracted for export, but, on the contrary,
unless things change very much, a large balance will still
have to come to India. As the mints would be closed to
silver, the greater portion of this balance would come in
gold, which would form a basis for the currency, and thus
lead to the establishment of a perfect system.

It might be well to point out that my proposal, though

* [See page 46 for the statement, which is there brought down to
31st March, 1897.]

arrived at by an entirely independent process of reasoning, is, I believe, in its ends in complete harmony with a suggestion made by Lord Sherbrooke in 1879. In an article published in the *Fortnightly Review* of July, in that year, the Right Honourable Robert Lowe, as he was then, suggested that the currency of the rupee should be limited to amounts of small value, and that a paper currency should be introduced to be sustained at par with gold by the right to require bullion for notes, and notes for bullion, in certain specified quantities. This was practically identical with Mr. Ricardo's proposal—for the issue of notes on the deposit of bullion—which was adopted in Sir Robert Peel's Bill for the resumption of cash payments in 1819. Mr. Lowe left the introduction of the system to such means as Indian experts might think best, and did not explain how he proposed to obtain the gold with which to start it. My proposal is, by beginning with the right to demand notes and silver rupees for gold bullion, to ultimately arrive at the stage when we shall be able also to give the right to demand gold bullion for notes and silver rupees.

It is outside the subject of this paper to discuss what effect the adoption of a gold standard by India would have on the value of gold in the world. India, I think, should take care of itself. It will be noticed that under my scheme any gold that may once get into the currency vaults in quantities smaller than 160 lbs. weight, will be kept there, and will form part of the reserve which will not be used until the currency corresponds to the standard. Unless gold be required for export (and the past history of Indian trade precludes the probability of this call) it will not command a premium in the market, and it is only reasonable to suppose that with the immense amount of gold scattered over the country in small quantities some

will find its way into the currency reserve. Then, too,
there are our Indian gold mines, and though these have
been in most cases hitherto unprofitable to the English *
investor gold is being produced in small quantities which
will probably come to the Treasury for exchange into
current money.   The production up to date is over
£200,000. *

The immediate effect of the closing of the Indian
mints on the price of council bills and the rate of Indian
exchange would be to raise them to the price at which
gold could be remitted to India after allowing for interest
and transit charges.   Thus, supposing we take these
charges at 2 per cent.,† the rate of exchange would be
18·36d. per rupee.   No one wanting to remit money to
India would give more; because it could be remitted at
that rate by the transmission of gold bullion.   The rate
would vary from day to day just as our exchanges vary
with other gold standard countries, but so long as the
demand for remittance to the East to adjust the balance
of Indian exports continues, the exchange would not fall
below specie point.   It would no doubt be the ruling
plan of the Secretary of State to sell his bills so cheaply
as to prevent the unnecessary flow of gold to India : but
unless the circumstances of trade altered very considerably
there would still be a tendency for bullion to go to India
for the final adjustment of the balance of trade.

So radical a change as the introduction of a gold
standard into India could not be carried out without being
open to many objections.   I will examine those which
occur to me, and those which have been advanced by
friends whom I have consulted, as dispassionately as
possible.

* [The production is now at the rate of about £1,400,000 a year.]
† [The charges are really only about ½ per cent.]

The adoption of my proposal, it is urged, would at once cause a further and serious fall in the gold price of silver. I admit that the shock at first to the silver market would be very great. I believe, however, that the price would ·in time adjust itself to the altered circumstances. The least profitable mines would be closed, and the least profitable modes· of working abandoned, when prices fell, and when the stimulus to production caused by the Indian mints being kept open for the general coinage of silver was removed. I have already dealt with the question of the intrinsic value of the rupee under my scheme compared with its nominal value as the token coin of a gold standard. With the rate which I have taken there would probably be no real danger in the extensive fabrication of illicit coins within Indian limits. The Government of India, when examining this objection in November, 1878, considered it of but little practical importance. The importation from abroad could be prevented by the imposition of heavy penalties.

The position of the American dollars, of the Latin Union five-franc pieces, and of our British token coinage, being so much worse than the position of the rupee at 1s. 6d., would be no doubt seriously affected.* But I am looking at the matter only *quâ* Indian interests. Possibly the case of the United States and the Latin Union might be so serious as to induce them to open their mints to silver at their old rates. If so, the difficulty would be solved. But, even in this case, if England and Germany thought it wise to adhere to their single gold standards, I would continue the gold standard for India, raising the rupee from $\frac{3}{40}$ of £1, as I have taken it in this paper, to something above its nominal gold value at the Latin

* [See table on page 31.]

Union rate, *viz.*, $\frac{2261}{24000}$ of £1—say to $\frac{2336}{24000}$ of £1, which is the rate of 15 to 1, recognised under the Indian Coinage Act, and which would be quite sufficient to prevent all chance of the currency being depleted for export after a gold standard had been established.

I have already alluded to the suggestion that the apparent fall in the value of silver caused by the rupee being taken at a fixed value in gold higher than its intrinsic value might cause discontent, and the more silver fell the greater would be the apparent loss, and the more serious would be the risk of discontent. On this point it may be opportune to quote the recorded opinion of the Government of India, in para. 69 of their despatch of 9th November, 1878 : " We think that no fairer subject of taxation could be found, if that expression rightly describes the effect of the change of standard, than the silver bullion virtually buried without producing any useful return to the country ". And it must be borne in mind that the longer action is postponed the more difficult does it become, the more serious will be the loss, the more grave the discontent. We are encouraging the hoarding of a metal every day decreasing in value. It has, I think, been admitted by all parties that there is a point, though this point may never have been precisely stated, below which the gold value of the rupee must not be allowed to fall. There has been much talk at times of rises and re-actions ; but the best opinions now point to a lower, rather than to a higher, level. As it is, our Government in India is troubled to find means to meet its liabilities. It appears to me that there is more likelihood of discontent from increased taxation to meet the loss caused by the fall in the gold value of silver than of discontent caused by the cheapness of the metal.

A more serious danger is the probability of the country

being flooded by hoards of rupees which would be brought out when their nominal value became materially in excess of their intrinsic worth. The scheme would, no doubt, act as an inducement to bring out hoards which might otherwise have remained dormant, and if it operated to any great extent in this direction it might bring about a redundancy of coin which, with a currency not capable of automatic contraction, might result in serious consequences. But, in the first place, allowance must be made for the additional coin required to meet the wants of the country caused by increased population and development, and, secondly, it should be remembered that the danger to some extent exists under our present system, and by encouraging the coinage of rupees, we are increasing its magnitude. It seems to me impossible that the present state of things can go on for ever; but that, even if the natives of India do not, to some extent, abandon their habits of hoarding generally, they will, sooner or later, and especially if the gold value of silver continue to fall, realise the mistake they are making in hoarding it. We shall then, even under our silver monometallic system, have their hoards thrown on the country, with the result of an enormous rise in prices, which would not only, like all sudden changes, be injurious to the public at large, and especially to a people so conservative in their habits and customs as the people of India are, but which would be most embarrassing to the Government, as a great part of the revenue is either permanently fixed or incapable of immediate expansion.

I do not think it has been sufficiently realised that the fact of prices not having risen in India as would be the expected result of the depreciation of the gold value of silver, is owing, in a great measure, to the quantity of silver which has been hoarded, and which of course, therefore, has no effect on the circulation of the country. The coinage at the Indian mints is no index whatever of the amount put into circulation; for not only is silver constantly hoarded in the form of rupees, but all over the country rupees are melted down for ornaments, since the convenience of using silver in this form and the guarantee afforded by the Government stamp compensate sufficiently for the cost of the seigniorage charged on their coinage.

Another objection is the danger of an over-issue of the monopoly silver coins by the Government, either inadvertently, or for the sake of the profit which would arise therefrom.* The real effectual safeguard against the over-issue of all tokens, is, as has been explained, an assurance of their redemption in full standard money. This assurance would be wanting on the first introduction of my scheme. But I believe that with publicity ensured by legislative enactment, and with the Government and the public alive as they would be to the danger of over-issue, there would be nothing to fear. There is no reason why the Government of India should in this matter act with less discretion than the Government of France; it is certain that the influences which have been brought to bear on the Government of the United States to secure the coinage of silver in excess of the requirements of the country will not operate in the case of the Government of India.

An objection to the scheme, and one which it will require some ingenuity to get over, is the difficulty of dealing with rupees which are now current in Ceylon, Mauritius, and elsewhere outside British India. Special legislation in concert with the colonies concerned would

---

* [In my subsequent scheme an automatic guard against this danger was adopted by making the amount of silver coinage depend on the composition of the metallic reserve of the currency department.]

be necessary; and I apprehend that a plan might be arranged for their adoption of a gold standard with a subsidiary currency of their own.*

It will be said, no doubt, that my scheme will involve additional demands on the gold stock of the world, and will result, therefore, in the still further appreciation of that metal, from which, according to some authorities, all countries are suffering so severely. I will not enter into the question as to how far the present depression of trade has been caused by the scarcity of gold. I will only remark that, in my humble opinion, more injury has been done by the alteration of prices caused by the deviations in the relative value of the two great standards of value than by the scarcity of one of them. But under my scheme the demand on the gold stock of the world will really not be very large. Some of it may, indeed, be met from the existing stocks of India. In any case, the matter should be regarded by the Indian Minister entirely from an Indian point of view. If the interests of India demand a gold standard, it should be adopted irrespectively of its effect on the world generally.

I have already dealt with what is no doubt the most formidable objection to the scheme, *viz.*: that the currency proposed is one which will not be strictly automatic in its action. Under my scheme provision is made for its automatic expansion to any extent, but no provision is made for its automatic contraction. I have endeavoured, however, to explain that, owing to the balance of trade being in favour of India, there is no likelihood of remittances of bullion from India, and consequent contraction

---

* [This has since been done with the small and comparatively unimportant colony of British Honduras; though I believe a mistake was made in converting the dollar at a much higher gold value than it had at the time of the change.]

of currency being necessary. In the course of time too, I hope that so much gold might be held by the currency department as would constitute a reserve which might enable the Government to undertake always to issue gold bars to the value of Rs. 100,000 (or one-lakh notes) in exchange for rupees or rupee notes presented for the purpose. When this state of things shall arise, not only would all possible fear of an excessive issue of *tokens* be avoided, but we should have a currency which would automatically contract as well as automatically expand—a currency which, to use the words of Lord Sherbrooke, would be "sustained at par with gold by the right to require bullion for notes, and notes for bullion in certain specified quantities".

It will no doubt be asked what particular advantage the gold standard, which has been recommended for India in this paper, has over the simpler standards combined with a gold currency which have been suggested by various authorities.

The Government of India in a despatch dated 9th November, 1878, to which reference has already been made, proposed the adoption of a gold standard and a gold currency in India at the rate of two shillings per rupee. It was proposed to do this by raising the seigniorage on the coinage of silver from time to time to such a rate as would virtually make the cost of a rupee, to persons importing bullion, equal to the tenth of a sovereign in gold. The late Colonel Smith, R.E., an officer of great ability, and who, as formerly Mint Master at Madras and Calcutta, had unusual opportunities for studying the subject, for many years before his death also very strongly advocated a gold standard and currency for India at the same rate. He proposed that the Indian mints should be closed for the coinage of silver of private individuals, and that gold sovereigns should be coined at the rate of 38 rupees 14 annas per standard ounce corresponding to a rupee for two Shillings. Probably with the further fall, which has since occurred, he would not have suggested so high a value to be put on silver rupees, which now means a greater difference between the nominal and intrinsic value of the token than it did. When he was writing in 1880, silver had never fallen so low as 49d. an ounce. Mr. William Douglas, a Glasgow gentleman, to whose writings on the subject I feel much indebted, also advocates a gold standard on the same principle as Colonel Smith, proposing to take the rupee at one-twelfth instead of at one-tenth of the £1. And a very high authority on Indian financial matters, whose opinion is of much greater value than mine, and who has seen my proposal, thinks that if a gold standard were to be introduced into India at the present time it would best be done by closing the Indian mints to silver, and making the gold mohur, or 15-rupee piece, a legal tender for 20 rupees. This would be adopting a ratio between gold and silver of 20 to 1.

Now, all these proposals appear to me to be open to the grave objection that they would postpone almost indefinitely the period at which the Government would be in a position to put the token currency on the sound healthy basis of being exchangeable into the standard ; as cannot be too strongly insisted on, the surest security against the abuse of a large token currency being its free convertibility into full standard metal. It is this end which should be held in view, whatever scheme may be adopted for linking silver with gold when the latter is the sole standard. And this end can only, I believe, be attained by using gold in the first instance, not as a currency, but as a reserve.

Not only would the demands for gold currency in a

country like India be very large, and until they were satisfied there would be no reserve of gold to draw on, but the establishment of a gold coinage would emphasise the taste which now exists for gold ornaments and hoarding.

Those of my hearers who have been in India know how much even the poorer classes delight in gold ornaments, and can imagine how with a gold currency their efforts would be constantly made in the direction of current gold coins for this use.   I myself have seen the child of one of my horsekeepers, drawing a wage of only six rupees a month, clothed with nothing but four gold 5-rouble pieces round his neck ; and the fondness of natives for gold ornaments is well known.   I do not say that under my plan they would be prevented from using gold for this purpose ; but I do say they would not be encouraged as they would be if gold were current money constantly passing from hand to hand.   And I contend that, when owing to times of pressure, or other circumstances, the gold in small quantities had passed into the currency vaults, it would be useful then as a reserve for the current circulation of the country which eventually might be built up to such an extent as to result in a perfect gold standard.   A very striking instance of the way in which hoards and jewels of gold will come into the market in India, was afforded by the memorable famine of 1877-79. I cannot now lay my hands on an interesting report which was issued by the Bombay mint on the subject, but the following figures, showing the export of gold from India during the decade 1875 to 1884,* are as eloquent as words :—

* [The statement has been brought down to March 31, 1897. The large shipments of silver to India following the Sherman Act, or made in anticipation of the closure of the mints, no doubt led to the large exports of gold between 1892 and 1895.   otherwise the increase in the exports is mainly the Indian gold mines and to the high rupee

VALUE OF GOLD EXPORTED FROM INDIA.
Official Years ending 31st March.

	Rx.			Rx.
1875	215,701	1887	. . . .	656,500
1876	291,250	1888	. . . .	243,600
1877	1,236,362	1889	. . . .	305,200
1878	1,110,798	1890	. . . .	455,700
1879	2,359,223	1891	. . . .	864,700
1880	299,889	1892	. . . .	1,705,100
1881	16,859	1893	. . . .	4,594,500
1882	12,408	1894	. . . .	2,505,300
1883	164,264	1895	. . . .	6,730,400
1884	6,141	1896	. . . .	2,503,300
1885	106,240	1897	. . . .	2,200,000
1886	328,600			

There can be no doubt but that if the mints had been closed to silver during the three years 1877 to 1879, and open to gold under arrangements such as I have suggested, the greater part of the £4,796,383 worth of gold exported in those years would have been kept in India in the currency reserve. God forbid that there should be another like period. But I believe that by arrangements such as I have indicated, we should get hold of much more gold even in seasons of much less pressure.*

I have purposely abstained from saying anything in this paper about the proposed bimetallic remedy. Though not myself in favour of bimetallism, I am quite sensible of the soundness of many of the arguments which have been advanced in its support, and I believe that if it could be adopted and maintained by the principal countries of the world, the evils from which India suffers would be more effectually removed than by the scheme which I have recommended. I trust, however, that any discussion which may follow the reading of this paper may be confined to a criticism of my proposal on its own merits, apart from its relative

* [Only of course on the hypothesis that the gold rate adopted became effective.]

value to any other plan for dealing with the currency
question. There is apparently no chance of either England or Germany giving their adherence to a bimetallic
convention ; and France and the United States of America
will therefore make no change in their present policy.
The time seems to me to have arrived when India should
do something for herself. She happens to be so circumstanced that in this matter she can almost dictate her
terms to the world, and it is for her rulers to see that
she exercises the power which she possesses, and demands and obtains what is best for her own interests.
The scheme which I have put before you in this paper
is one which could be carried out by India without any
extraneous aid, without any consultation with foreign
Powers. I propose it, believing that if it be adopted it
will conduce to the prosperity and welfare of the many
millions of our fellow-subjects whose interests it is the
paramount object of the East India Association to protect.

A GOLD STANDARD FOR INDIA (1892).

(Read before the Institute of Bankers, on 7th December, 1892.)

THE appointment of a Commission, presided over by
Lord Herschell, to consider whether any alterations
should be made in the currency arrangements of India,
gives the question as to the possibility of the introduction of a gold standard into that country a practical
importance. And, the welfare of India and England
being so closely bound together, the bankers of London,
apart from the direct effect which any alteration of the
Indian may have on the British standard of value, can
hardly afford to look on the matter with indifference.
From a purely Indian point of view, too, it is very
fortunate that an opportunity has been afforded by the
Institute of Bankers for the discussion of this important
subject, before a body of practical men, whose verdict
on a practical question must be of the greatest value.

We have been so long accustomed to think of India
as a country with a rupee currency, that the important
part taken by gold in its former monetary arrangements
is forgotten.   The unit of the Hindoo system of currency
was of gold, and, although the Mohammedan conquerors
introduced a silver rupee in 1542, gold still formed part
of the currency, while in the southern states, where they
did not gain ascendancy, a gold currency continued in
force, even after the British conquest. Thus, we find
that in 1796 gold pagodas, worth $3\frac{1}{2}$ rupees each, formed

the principal part of the remittance annually made from Madras to Bengal; and gold still circulates to some extent in Southern India. There was, indeed, a large coinage of silver between 1801 and 1833, but it was not till 1835 that the present coinage system, under which silver became the sole legal tender of value in British India, was established.

At present the money of British India consists of rupees coined in 1835 and subsequently, unlimited legal tender, for conversion into which bullion is received from all comers at a charge of one per mille for melting, and 2 per cent. seigniorage: of half, quarter and eighth of rupees, of the same fineness and proportionate weight as the rupee—the half rupee, though full legal tender, being only used as small change, and the quarter and eighth of rupees being only legal tender for fractions of a rupee: of copper coins, likewise, only legal tender for fractions of a rupee: and of Government currency notes.

The Indian paper currency system, which supplies the only note circulation in the country, was introduced in 1861. Notes are issued on the deposit of uncoined silver * or rupees. The Government is also empowered, after six months' notice, to " fix the rates, rules and conditions at, and according to, which gold may be taken in exchange for Government promissory notes " not exceeding one-fourth of the total issues: this power has not yet been exercised. Rx. 8,000,000 * is invested in Government securities, and coin or bullion is held to meet the whole circulation above that sum. India is divided into eight circles, and each circle has an office of issue situated at its principal town. From these offices notes of the denominations of 5, 10, 20, 50, 100, 500, 1000, 10,000 rupees, are issued in exchange for coin; they are by law

* [Modified in June, 1893. For present law see pp. 102-110.]

convertible into coin at the office of issue, and at the
office at the headquarters of the Presidency (Calcutta,
Bombay or Madras) in which the circle is situated.
They are legal tender in their respective circles of issue
alone ; but, as they are everywhere accepted in payment
of Government demands, and generally encashable at all
Government treasuries, they circulate to a great extent
independent of the circle to which they belong.   Their
convertibility is facilitated by the general treasury system,
and by a rule allowing portions of the reserve of the
paper currency department to be held at certain Government treasuries (at present sixty in number) in separate
" currency chests " under strict regulations securing their
contents for this service.   During the year ended 31st
March, 1892, notes were cashed " to the full extent of the
public demand" at 164 out of 243 treasuries ; they were
" ordinarily cashed, but not always " at 48 ; while only at
31 they were " not usually cashed".   Besides the notes
of home circles thus cashed at treasuries, during the
same year notes of other circles amounting to nearly
Rx. 6,000,000 were cashed at currency offices not legally
bound to cash them.   The continued expansion of this
class of business, points to the early adoption of a uni-
versal note, encashable by law at four or five of the
principal towns of the empire ; a measure which would
add greatly to the popularity of the notes without very
materially adding to the responsibility, which the Government now voluntarily undertakes.   " Notes of Rs. 100 and
under are gradually making their way into every corner
of the empire, and beyond it, into Central Asia and even
parts of Africa." *   Traders from Afghanistan frequently
take back their earnings from India in this form.   And
though largely employed for the purposes of storing

* Report of Commissioner of Currency for 1891-92.

money, and for remittances, the use of notes is extending
in the retail transactions of the country. Thus, ten rupee
notes constitute no less than 68 per cent. of the number,
and 15 per cent. of the value of the total circulation. The
average circulation during the last ten years, and the
denominations of the notes outstanding at the end of
each of the last three years, are given below. The increase which took place in the year 1890-91 was due to
the large import of silver into India, consequent on
American legislation.

AVERAGE VALUE OF GOVERNMENT CURRENCY NOTES IN CIRCULATION
THROUGHOUT INDIA, IN TENS OF RUPEES.*

1882-83	15,180,711
1883-84	13,386,926
1884-85	14,540,727
1885-86	14,710,203
1886-87	14,201,095
1887-88	16,162,329
1888-89	16,431,629
1889-90	16,151,496
1890-91	22,889,227
1891-92	25,436,237
1892-93	27,099,563
1893-94	28,291,524
1894-95	31,111,140
1895-96	29,281,029
Actual March 31, 1897	23,753,307

VALUE OF NOTES OF DIFFERENT DENOMINATIONS IN CIRCULATION AT THE
CLOSE OF EACH YEAR, IN TENS OF RUPEES.*

Denomina-tion.	31st March, 1893.	31st March, 1894.	31st March, 1895.	31st March, 1896.	31st March, 1897.
Rs.					
5	247,728	249,826	281,507	312,776	
10	3,917,236	3,744,939	4,929,358	4,600,900	
20	660,166	664,046	729,800	736,178	
50	1,162,410	1,009,140	1,201,375	1,238,195	
100	5,680,680	5,192,480	6,171,920	6,227,850	
500	2,532,400	2,119,500	2,393,250	2,460,700	
1,000	6,798,100	5,381,800	6,116,800	6,649,100	
10,000	5,403,000	11,960,000	9,477,000	3,715,000	
Total	26,401,820	30,411,631	30,700,010	25,940,699	23,753,307

* [These tables have been as far as possible completed to 31st March,
1897.]

Under the Indian Coinage Act, the mints are bound *
to coin gold into 5, 10, 15 or 30 rupee gold-pieces, at a
charge of ¼ per mille for melting, and 1 per cent. for
seigniorage, but these coins are not legal tender. They
may, however, be paid into Government treasuries for their
nominal amount, but this option is never exercised, the
valuation of gold to silver in these coins being at the rate
of 15 to 1, against 15½ to 1, the old Latin Union rate,
and something like 25 to 1, the present market rate.†

STATEMENT SHOWING THE GOLD VALUE OF SILVER IN THE RUPEE, AT
VARIOUS PROPORTIONS OF GOLD TO SILVER, AND AT VARIOUS
GOLD PRICES OF STANDARD SILVER.

Proportion-ate Value of Gold to Silver.	Gold Price in Pence of an Ounce of Standard Silver.	Gold Value in Pence of Silver in the Rupee.	Remarks.
39·71	23·75	8·83	The lowest price of silver yet reached.
32·35	29·15	10·83	Japanese rate of conversion.
28·58	33·	12·26	Half British token rate. Intrinsic value of shilling 1/20 of £1.
24·87	38·	14·12	
23·36	40·36	15·	Rate suggested in this paper.
23·25	40·56	15·07	Russian silver rouble under new law.
21·90	43·06	16·	Rate at which Indian treasuries are authorised to receive gold by notifi-cation of June, 1893.
20·61	45·75	17·	⎫ Various rates suggested.
20·	47·15	17·52	⎬
19·47	48·43	18·	⎭
16·	58·79	21·90	American dollar rate.
15·5	60·84	22·61	Latin Union rate.
15·	62·87	23·36	Gold mohur. Indian Coinage Act.
14·97	62·99	23·41	£1=Rs. 10 as. 4.
14·6	64·59	24·	So-called old par rate.
14·29	66·	24·53	British token rate.

Orders, too, were issued in 1864, under which sovereigns
and half-sovereigns were to be received at the rate of Rs.

* [Modified in June, 1893.]
† The above statement will serve to illustrate the foregoing and
subsequent remarks. [Some additions have been made to the statement
as originally printed.]

10 annas 4, and Rs. 5 annas 2 respectively ; but as at this rate gold is even less valued compared with silver than it is in the 15-rupee piece of the Coinage Act, the orders, though still I believe unrepealed, have remained a dead letter.*

The question of the amount of money circulating in India is one of great importance and considerable complexity. The matter, however, has been gone into very carefully by Mr. Harrison, a young officer of the Bengal Civil Service—at present Deputy Accountant-General of Bengal—in two articles in the *Economic Journal* in December, 1891, and June, 1892. The conclusions at which he arrives may, I think, be accepted. He estimated the money in circulation in British India and feudatory states using British Indian money at Rx. 134,170,000, for a population of 236,550,000, working out an average of Rs. 5·67 per head.

This average is thus distributed :—

	Rupees.
Rupees ...	4·09
Currency Notes	1·
Small Silver ...	·30
Copper ...	·19
Gold	·09
	5·67

The above figures include the various kinds of money held by Government treasuries and banks,† but not the specie reserve of the currency department, and indicate the important part now taken by paper in the circulation of the country.

* [Altered in June, 1893 ; see page vii.]

† The proportion of currency notes held by the Government treasuries and banks is larger than that held outside ; the proportion in *bonâ fide* circulation among the people was not, therefore, quite so great as these figures indicate.

The treasury system of India affords the Government great opportunities for carrying out its monetary policy. There are 243 treasuries and a much larger number of sub-treasuries, at each of which revenue is received, sometimes in small sums and from a great number of people, and from each of which disbursements are made on Government account. These treasuries and sub-treasuries, besides facilitating the circulation of currency notes, as has been already explained, exercise important functions in regard to the token, or representative money. As the proposals which I shall have to submit for your consideration depend upon what I consider the true function of a Government in regard to its representative money being admitted, I must trouble you with some elementary details on this subject. Mr. Goschen once, rather happily as I think, called our British representative coins "*metallic notes*". An old Manx silver token * which I have seen bears on it the inscription : "The Douglas Bank Company at their Bank, Douglas, promise to pay the bearer on demand 5 shillings British, 1811". I submit respectfully that, though the direct promise in the legend may be unnecessary, every Government issuing representative money should undertake the responsibility implied by it. Our British shillings and florins should be, like the old tokens, promises of the issuer—that is to say of the mint—to pay the bearer on demand $\frac{1}{20}$ and $\frac{1}{10}$ of a sovereign respectively. It is a similar responsibility, in respect to its representative money, which the Government of India, though not legally bound to do so, undertakes. For not only are all sums due to the Government receivable in full in all its token coins, but the treasuries and sub-treasuries exchange full standard for token coins, and *vice versá*, for all comers.

---

* Weighing 233 grains, and with an intrinsic value, even at 66 pence an ounce, of only 32 pence.

In this respect I believe that the Government of India does its duty better than any other Government in the world, with the result that the standard and representative coins are kept at par with each other all over the country, and that the complaints which occasionally are heard even in England (where the Government duty is so well done by the banks) of scarcity of small change are unknown. With such arrangements—with the free convertibility of representative money into the standard substance—even without the limited legal tender property, there can be no fear of representative coins interfering with the efficiency of the standard. The limited legal tender safeguard is of small consequence, provided over-issue is guarded against by free convertibility.

It is not proposed to examine in detail the evils said to have arisen from India having a silver standard of valuation, but the causes which appear to make a change advisable must be briefly alluded to. They are as follows :—

1. The injury to trade between gold-using countries and India caused by the uncertain gold value of the rupee. About 80 per cent. of the total external trade of India is with gold-using countries.

2. The hindrance to the flow of capital to India caused by the apparent uncertainty which the gold investor feels as to his profits realisable in silver, and by the absolute uncertainty as to the value at which he will be able ultimately to withdraw his gold capital.

3. The encouragement of the flow of silver to India for speculative purposes merely, rather than for the legitimate requirements of trade and investment.

4. The encouragement of the acceptance, for hoards and ornaments by the people of India, of a metal which is falling in value in the general markets of the world.

5. The rise of silver prices which must sooner or later

follow if the fall in the gold value of silver goes on; a disturbing element which, though it might benefit some, would injure other members of the community.

6. The injury to the State owing to the increased amount of silver money which a further fall in the value of that metal will necessitate for its gold payments. Assuming the exchange at 1s. 3d. the rupee, and the gold payment at £16,000,000 per annum, the "loss by exchange" is Rx. 9,600,000. But with further falls the loss goes on increasing with alarming rapidity. A fall of one penny means an additional amount of Rx. 1,828,571; of threepence, Rx. 6,400,000.

7. The higher interest the Government has to pay on silver than on gold loans. Roughly there is a difference of 1 per cent.

8. The increased salaries which will have to be paid to the European employees of the Government to maintain their efficiency irrespective of any claim they may have in equity.

9. The general uncertainty of prices of certain agricultural produce and manufactured goods in gold-using countries, attributable more or less to the uncertain gold value of the rupee.

10. The disadvantage of the money markets of India and Europe being independent of each other, owing to their having different standards of valuation.

The sense in which it is proposed to use the term "standard" on the present occasion should be explained. Mr. Dana Horton, in his interesting work *The Silver Pound*, gives no less than nine meanings attached to the word when used in monetary discussions; but no one of these meanings expresses with sufficient clearness the term as I propose to use it. I venture, therefore, to offer for your consideration the following statement:

A country has a perfect gold monetary standard when its money is referable to a fixed gold unit; when all its money can be readily exchanged for gold with which it is thus sustained at par; when gold is the substance which alone the Government mints are bound to accept for conversion into current money; when all money bargains are based on gold, and expressed in gold or its efficient representatives; and when gold thus becomes the legal and effective measure of value.

To illustrate this statement by two typical cases of countries belonging to the Latin Union : (a) Italy would not under it be classed as a country with a gold monetary standard ; for though the law admits of gold being the unrestricted measure of value, and though for some time after the resumption of specie payments, her circulating medium was kept at par with gold, this is at present not the case ; and gold, measured in Italian currency, again commands a premium. (b) France, on the other hand, still has a gold monetary standard ; for notwithstanding the large stocks of silver held as full legal tender money, the whole circulating medium, including silver, is practically exchangeable into and sustained at par with gold, and gold is the only metal which can be freely coined into legal tender money.

There are other countries recognised generally as gold standard countries which, owing to the practical difficulty of exchanging the current money for gold, hardly come under my somewhat rigid definition. But for my present purpose this is a fault on the right side. I wish the standard at which I am aiming for India to be free from these imperfections.

Because a country has a gold monetary standard it does not follow that gold forms the principal, or indeed any, part of the circulating medium. Thus in the United

States of America gold scarcely circulates at all, the current transactions being carried out by paper of various
descriptions, at present sustained at par with gold by
different devices; and—a less important, though perhaps
more striking, instance—in Canada, not only is there
practically no gold in circulation, but, though the maintenance at par of the circulating medium is ensured by the
"Dominion Notes" being convertible into gold at the
place at which they are made payable, the ultimate reserve of gold in the country in proportion to the circulation is insignificant.   One more illustration of a homely
character: an important part of the circulating medium
of Scotland is paper which, though not even legal tender,
passes from hand to hand in settlement of perhaps the
bulk of the retail transactions of the country, without
interfering in any way with the gold standard of value.
These cases sufficiently illustrate my remark that it is not
necessary for a country with a gold standard, according to
the definition given, to have a gold circulation.

Stress has been laid on this point because the possibility
of the introduction of a gold standard into India depends
on its recognition.   For though India is spoken of as a
poor country, the value of silver either circulating as
money, or hoarded or formed into ornaments, must be
very large.   If gold became an important part of the circulating medium, as well as the standard, much of this
silver would be displaced by it.   Not only would gold be
more convenient for the larger payments, and more easily
concealed and hoarded, but, being the standard metal,
every one would try to get ornaments and hoards in that
form.   The quantity of gold required to supply the void
would be enormous.   To use Prince Bismarck's illustration: "The struggle for the blanket would be terrific".
If before the standard of India were changed from silver

to gold it were necessary to provide sufficient gold to meet circulation requirements, even if there were no smaller gold-piece than the sovereign, we should probably have to wait, if not till the discovery of the philosopher's stone, at any rate until the sanguine expectations of the promoters of gold-mining companies during the last few years had been fully realised. For, though the general tendency to hoarding is diminishing, I cannot share the opinion of my friend Mr. Clarmont Daniell, whose proposal for the free coinage of both gold sovereigns and silver rupees and their circulation side by side at their relative market rates, to be notified from time to time by the authorities, was discussed before this Institute in 1886, that the recognition of gold as money in India would draw out the hoards of that metal which undoubtedly exist.

Many other proposals have been made in the past for the adoption of a gold standard with a gold currency, which have justly excited the apprehension of those who view with alarm the appreciation of gold which has already taken place. The proposals of Colonel Smith in 1876, of the Government of India in 1878, and of Mr. William Douglas in 1879, were of this character. It is understood, too, that both Mr. McKay,* the President of the Indian Currency Association, and Sir David Barbour, think that if a gold standard be introduced, provision should be made for a gold currency as well. Other proposals, however, have been made for the introduction of a gold standard without a gold currency. A writer† in the *Bankers' Magazine* for August put forward an elaborate plan, which claims to be founded on Ricardo's scheme, and which was said to have been supported by all the Calcutta leading papers. Instead, however, of the gold bars ‡ contemplated by Ricardo, the only gold reserve for

* [Now Sir James McKay, K.C.I.E.]   † [Mr. Lindsay.]   ‡ [Or bullion.]

the Indian monetary system was to be that held by the
issue department of the Bank of England, which was to
be reduced by the bank exercising its option of holding
one fifth of it in silver. This plan will certainly not com-
mend itself to the Bankers' Institute. Proposals have
also been made for the adoption of a gold standard without
any gold basis at all, either by the simple closure of the
mints to silver, leaving the rupee to be worked up to, and
maintained at, a suitable gold rate by its monopoly character; or by the imposition of a fixed or varying seigniorage with the same object; or by the charge of such a
heavy import duty on silver as shall bring that metal in
India up to its required gold value. Without discussing
the demerits of these several schemes, I will content myself by observing that they do not come within the
definition of a gold monetary standard, which I have
ventured to lay down.

There is one more proposal which I will explain, and
it is one with which the proposal I shall presently submit
for your consideration is in harmony. The late Lord
Sherbrooke—then Mr. Lowe—in the debate on the Indian
Budget in the House of Commons on the 23rd May, 1879,
and in the *Fortnightly Review* of July in that year, suggested that a paper currency founded on gold, according
to Ricardo's plan, should be introduced, the currency of
the rupee being limited to amounts of small value, and
the paper currency being sustained at par with gold by
the right to require bullion for notes, and notes for bullion
in certain specified quantities.

The basis of Lord Sherbrooke's, as it was of Mr.
Ricardo's proposal, was that if the exchange of the current
money of a country into the standard substance could be
guaranteed and *vice versâ*, the standard substance would
act efficiently as a measure of value, even though it was

not used at all as current money.   This principle is also
the basis of my proposal.

It is, indeed, the same principle which I have stated[*]
in another form, when saying that the efficiency of representative coins as a measure of value, depends rather upon
their convertibility than on their limited legal tender property.   My proposition is to establish a gold unit of
valuation in India ; to provide for silver rupees constituting
as at present the chief part of the current money of the
country ; to encourage in every way the extension of paper
currency ; to gradually replace the bulk of the silver
reserve of the Currency Department with gold ; thus to
build up a gold reserve, which shall not only be the basis
of the paper currency, but which shall also to some
extent be security for the difference between the intrinsic
and nominal gold values of the silver representative coins ;
to allow no further increase to the stock of such coins
without setting apart gold to meet the difference between
their intrinsic and nominal gold values ; and to arrange
gradually for the convertibility into gold of rupees and
notes, so that if, owing to the state of trade or other
circumstances, representative money becomes redundant,
it may be automatically withdrawn by exchange into the
standard substance.

Before detailing the plans for giving effect to this proposition, it will be best to discuss what gold value should
be assigned to the present circulating medium, and what
should be the value of the gold unit.

First.—As to the gold value to be assigned to the
present silver circulating medium.   The rate which
appears on the whole most suitable is to take the silver
rupee as worth $\frac{1}{15}$ of £1.[*]   This would have the advan-

* This represents a proportion of 23·96 of silver to 1 of gold, or standard silver at 40·36d. per ounce. See table, p. 31.

tage of simplicity ; it could be easily adapted to our British system of valuation ; it would lend itself readily to arithmetical calculations ; and it would be understood by the people of India. There would be no very great change in the present value, which though now less than $\frac{1}{16}$ of £1, has till lately ruled considerably higher. Unless there were a general agreement on the part of the leading monetary nations to open mints to the free coinage of both metals at a rate more favourable to silver, there would be no likelihood of any rise in the gold value of the rupee beyond this rate. And on the other hand, though in the first instance the stoppage of the demand for rupee coinage would cause a serious further fall in the value of silver, we might hope that this would in time right itself, and that silver would probably settle down at a price not so much below 40·36d.* per ounce, as to give sufficient encouragement to the illicit fabrication of coins of full fineness.

Second.—What should the Indian gold unit be ? As the object is to retain the existing circulating medium, the gold unit should be so large as to be unavailable for circulation itself. Probably a gold unit of 160 oz. 10 dwts. 6·54375 grains of British standard gold,† representing 10,000 rupees or £625, would, as an initial measure, meet the case.

I am prepared to be told that it is too large to secure the free convertibility of representative money. A smaller unit would no doubt be better ; and, if the plan succeeded, its ultimate adoption should certainly (as I shall explain) be aimed at ; but the object is gradually to build up a

* The intrinsic gold value of British silver money has fallen more than 60 per cent. below its value as the representative of gold.

† See Mint Report, 1888. It is possible to deal satisfactorily with much larger ingots.

gold reserve ; and the higher the unit the more prospect there is of doing this, and of the early realisation of the scheme. •

It would be necessary to pass an Act with the following provisions:—

The legal standard to be declared to be ingots of gold eleven-twelfths pure, weighing 160 oz. 10 dwts. 6˙54375 grains ; the equivalent of £625 or Rs. 10,000 ; the mints to be closed to the free coinage of silver, thus restricting the use of that metal as money to the coins already in existence, or which might hereafter be struck on Government account ; these coins to be declared still full legal tender as representatives of $\frac{1}{10000}$ part of the gold unit ; the mints to be required to make gold brought to them, without any charge if in the form of full weight British gold coins, subject to a small charge for melting and refining, if in any other form, into these gold ingots ; the Currency Department and all treasuries and sub-treasuries acting for it, to be authorised to give rupees or notes in exchange for sovereigns, and for other gold in quantities of not less than say 2 oz., subject to a small charge for melting and refining ; such gold being held as part of the ordinary currency reserve.   The present 10,000-rupee notes of the Currency Department to be called in, and in future notes of Rs. 10,000, payable at the option of the holder either in gold, or silver rupees, to be issued in exchange for gold alone ; gold in the form of the standard ingots being specially reserved to meet every such note outstanding.   The gold, other than that set apart for the gold notes, to be held as part of the ordinary currency reserve, until the amount held in silver became less than one-half of the reserve of gold and silver combined, in which case the gold * might, at the option of the Govern-

* [It would have been better if, instead of gold, the words "cash

ment, be used for the purchase and coinage of silver to
bring up the silver proportion to one-half. The Government to be empowered, at any time after this silver
proportion had, continuously for a period of say one
year, amounted to not more than one-half of the said
metallic reserve, to declare that rupees shall be legal
tender for payments up to Rs. 10,000 only, simultaneously
undertaking that the Currency Department shall give
standard gold ingots in exchange for rupees presented for
the purpose. The Government to be further empowered
at any subsequent period to call in the notes of Rs. 1000,
and to put them on a similar gold basis ; reducing the
size of the gold unit accordingly.*

    With such an enactment, the money of the country
would in the first instance consist of currency notes
exchangeable into silver rupees ; of a limited number of
silver rupees full legal tender but representing one-six-
teenth part of a sovereign ; and of small change as at
present. If owing to rupees being brought out of hoards,
or being imported from abroad, or being illicitly manufactured, the currency became redundant, the exchange
would fall below the established gold par fifteen pence,
and the only remedy would be for the Government to
reduce the redundancy by purchase. If, however, this did
not happen, and if the balance of trade continued in
favour of India as it has been in the past, the rupee
would be worth fifteen pence, subject to ordinary ex-

reserve " had been used in the text. When the composition of the cash
reserve permitted, and circumstances indicated the necessity for, increased
rupee coinage the silver bought for coinage would probably be paid for by
notes which would of course be exchangeable into coined rupees. For
illustration, see Appendix, page 52. See also Section 14 of Draft Bill,
page 118.]

    * The unit would then be a little over 16 oz. 1 dwt. of gold. 20 oz.
was the *minimum* suggested by Ricardo for the sale and purchase of gold.

change fluctuations, and the demand for an expansion of the currency could only be satisfied by gold being brought to the Currency Department. The expansion* would take one or other of the following forms :—*

(a) Either an issue of gold notes absolutely protected by an equivalent amount of gold.

(b) An increase in the silver circulation, accompanied by some part of the paper currency reserve being changed from silver to gold ; and, if it went on, by the difference between the actual cost of procuring additional silver coins, and their nominal gold value, accumulating in addition to the ordinary currency reserve.

(c) An increase in the ordinary note circulation, such increase being represented by gold held as part of the currency reserve.

There would be no fear of inconvenience owing to the reduction of the silver bullion reserve, for if gold came in too fast, the efficiency of the new standard would be proved. Any inconvenience might be at once remedied by giving gold in exchange for silver ; and, if necessary, by issuing gold notes of lower denominations.

I admit that the plan proposed would in the first instance result in an imperfect system. Until the Government undertook to give gold in exchange for its silver and paper, the standard would not be automatic ; until it was able to reduce the gold unit to a bar considerably smaller than the one I have suggested to commence with, the terms of my definition of a perfect gold standard would not be fulfilled. The standard would in the first instance be an *etalon boiteux* supported

* For illustration, see Appendix, page 52.

by monopoly rupees. Such a standard has, indeed, been seriously proposed as a permanent arrangement without the prospective gold backing at which I am aiming. No doubt, owing to the peculiar circumstances of the trade of India, she is in a very strong position for the maintenance of such a standard if a reasonable rate were fixed; but, though I take advantage of this position for the intermediate stage between silver and gold, and for ultimately acquiring the latter, I am as sensible as any one of the evils of a so-called metallic standard with only monopoly coins. The Government of India is, perhaps, strong enough to secure the gold to start with, but to do so would cause serious embarrassment and loss, to say nothing of the trouble which would result in European monetary circles—a trouble which would be immensely lessened if the provision of gold were left, as I propose, to the natural requirements of trade.

The following statement shows the net imports of gold and silver into India during the last twenty years :—*

* [The net imports for the five years 1892-93 to 1896-97 have been added. It should be borne in mind that since the closure of the mint in June, 1893, the rupee represents a much larger quantity of silver than it did formerly; and that the gradually increasing output from the Indian gold mines has tended to reduce the net imports of gold.]

NET IMPORTS (AFTER DEDUCTING EXPORTS) OF GOLD AND SILVER
INTO INDIA.

Year ending 31st March.	Gold.	Silver.	Total.
	Rx.	Rx.	Rx.
1873	2,543,362	715,144	3,258,506
1874	1,382,639	2,495,824	3,878,463
1875	1,873,535	4,642,203	6,515,738
1876	1,545,131	1,555,355	3,100,486
1877	207,350	7,198,872	7,406,222
1878	468,129	14,676,334	15,144,463
1879	—896,173	3,970,694	3,074,521
1880	1,750,504	7,869,743	9,620,247
1881	3,655,199	3,890,574	7,545,773
1882	4,843,984	5,379,050	10,223,034
1883	4,930,871	7,480,227	12,411,098
1884	5,462,505	6,405,152	11,867,657
1885	4,671,936	7,245,631	11,917,567
1886	2,762,935	11,606,629	14,369,564
1887	2,177,100	7,155,700	9,332,800
1888	2,992,481	9,228,751	12,221,232
1889	2,813,934	9,246,679	12,060,613
1890	4,615,303	10,937,876	15,553,179
1891	5,636,172	14,175,136	19,811,308
1892	2,413,800	9,022,200	11,436,000
1893	—2,812,700	12,863,600	10,050,900
1894	641,200	13,719,800	14,361,000
1895	—4,974,100	6,329,200	1,355,100
1896	2,526,000	6,582,200	9,108,200
1897	2,291,038	5,856,030	8,147,068

For the twenty years, then, there was an annual average net import into India of £2,792,535 in gold, and Rx. 7,244,889 in silver. With a change of standard this silver remittance, representing at 1s. 8d. £4,528,056, would go to India in gold.* The alteration, if it made any difference in the balance of trade† (I am supposing, of

* [This prediction was not fulfilled. It was only made, however, on the hypothesis of a definite scheme for a gold standard at "a rate corresponding nearly to the present rate," whereas there was no such scheme, and the rate temporarily authorised was 1¼d. above the then existing rate. The continued absorption of silver by India for ornaments after the mints were closed was not too foreseen.]

† By "balance of trade" I mean the balance of indebtedness which has to be adjusted by the remittance of bullion, and which, to use the

course, the adoption of a rate corresponding nearly to the
present rate), would make it more in favour of India. For
there probably would be an increased investment of
European capital, and the Government would find it
more prudent than in the past to raise its loans for public
works, etc., in Europe ; both cases involving increased
gold remittances. If there were a diminution in the net
excess of exports over imports, or in the investments held
by Europe in India, or if there were an increase in the
Council Bills and private remittances to Europe, it would
tell the other way. The possibility of some gold being
collected in India itself should not be ignored. The
scheme provides for the gathering of small quantities, and
for their retention when once obtained. It is undoubted
that if such a scheme had been in force during the
terrible famine of 1877-78, considerable quantities would
have been obtained. Our Indian gold mines, too, are now
realising £500,000* a year, which might be made available
for India with proper mint facilities.

I have already alluded to a possible redundancy of currency caused by the further fall in the gold value of silver
if a gold standard were adopted. The representative
rupee would probably be very seriously overrated even
with the low gold value assigned to it. If silver fell only
to 30d. an ounce, its intrinsic value would be only 11d.,
against 15d., its nominal value. Hoards would come out,
and it is impossible to say, without experiment, what
expansion of the rupee circulation might not thereby be
caused. Exchange might thus fall below the price fixed,
and the currency would be at a discount until the redundancy had worked off. It would be a grave disaster, and

words of Mr. Goschen, " depends upon the transactions which have to be
settled, not upon those which, by common consent, are held in abeyance
for a long term of years ".   * [Now £1,400,000.]

could only be immediately remedied by the Government, at great expense, withdrawing the redundancy. But I hope that the danger is not a real one. Mr. Harrison, in' the paper to which I have already alluded, estimates this hoarding at the rate of Rx. 500,000 a year. For fifty-eight years this represents Rx. 29,000,000—not a very unmanageable amount, for it is probable that the hoards, which are believed to be principally held in large quantities by men of wealth and position, would only come out gradually.

The same thing would be brought about, too, by the return from foreign countries—Ceylon, Mauritius and elsewhere — of the rupees accepted there as standard money. But with some ingenuity and arrangement with these colonies, this difficulty might be got over. And there is the danger of illicit coinage which would be induced by the high profit and the facility of putting such coins into circulation in a country where they formed the bulk of the circulating medium. Competent judges, however, think the Indian police strong enough to cope with this danger.

A more serious result might arise from the natives of India, who have been accustomed, for the last half-century at any rate, to look on their silver ornaments as a cash reserve—a reserve which they could always turn into money either by sale or pledging—finding that their silver had gone down in the recognised money of the country. Not only is there injustice in thus lowering the value of the metal which our monetary policy has induced these natives of India to purchase—an injustice for which it is difficult to devise any direct compensation*— but it may be a source of political danger. There may,

* It might perhaps be impossible, at any rate at first, to protect the silver in India by the imposition of an import duty. [A 5 per cent. import duty was imposed in 1894.]

however, be greater injustice in still encouraging the
flow of the still depreciating metal into India; and a
greater political danger in the increased taxation which
must be levied to meet the future losses which the maintenance of a silver standard will involve.

The further fall in the value of silver, which would
follow the adoption of a gold standard by India, would be
attended with evils outside that country which it would
not be right on the present occasion to ignore. As it is,
our silver representative coins are too highly rated. The
intrinsic value of the shilling at 38d. an ounce is less than
7d.; much too large a margin for safety. If silver fell to
33d., it would be 6d. It appears to me that, no matter
what India may do, England must sooner or later face
this question. There is another way in which it is thought
England may suffer if India were to adopt a gold standard.
Mr. Charles Hoare estimates that it would result in a
further appreciation of gold by about 20 per cent.! The
question of the appreciation of gold is a very com-
plicated one, which has been discussed by this Institute
on several occasions. I remember being very much struck
on one occasion when it was my privilege to be present,
by a remark made by Mr. William Fowler, that "the fall
of prices is a fall mainly due to the ingenuity of man".
It has seemed to me, looking at the articles from which
the index number of prices is arrived at, that the alterations in many of them are most distinctly due to the
cause mentioned by Mr. Fowler. It seems to me that
the amount of the standard substance required to regulate
the currency of solvent countries, which do not use
that substance in any great degree as current money,
is really very small, and that if a remedy for the past
and a security against further appreciation of gold be
desired, it should take the form of restricting the use of

4

gold as currency in Europe, rather than of preventing
India using it as the standard of value.   But I feel I
have no right to offer you my opinions on this subject..
I have only ventured to do so as a protest against what
seems to me the exaggerated effect which has been predicted in the event of a change of standard in India being
adopted.

It will be seen that under the scheme which I have
suggested the demand for gold has been reduced to a
minimum, and the *maximum* employment has been
found for silver.   The scheme is one which will be
gradual in its operation, and, I venture to think, will
be attended with less disturbance both in India and
England than any other effective scheme for a gold
standard which has yet been brought forward.   That
to a certain extent it is tentative I admit; and that a
really effective standard will not be introduced until
sufficient gold has been drawn into the Indian reserves
to warrant the Government in undertaking to set it free
should it be required, owing to the redundancy of the
circulation or an adverse balance of trade; but I believe
that this position would soon be reached with the large
gold unit I have suggested, and if so, the reduction of the
unit to Rs. 1000 would be only a matter of time.   When
this position had been reached ; when the Government of
India had accepted a legal responsibility to give to all
comers at certain principal towns in the Empire Rs. 1000
gold bars in exchange for 1000 silver rupees, or for a
corresponding amount of notes ; when in addition to this
legal obligation it was generally able to afford similar
facilities at all its treasuries, the perfect gold standard
at which I have aimed would have been secured.

I know that the plan which I have been privileged to
lay before you this evening will meet with many objectors.

It will not satisfy my many Indian friends, dependent on
a rupee income, who clamour not unreasonably for it to
be raised to a higher figure.   But if the money of India
be placed on a sound and satisfactory footing it will be an
easy matter to meet their just claims.   And it will be
objected to by those who think it possible that an international agreement can be arrived at for the coinage of
both gold and silver at a fixed ratio ; and by those who
attribute all our troubles to the appreciation of gold.   But
both classes will probably admit that the scheme is more
desirable than the gold standard with a gold currency,
which has such powerful advocates.   At any rate I
present my proposal as an honest endeavour, on the
part of one who has been occupied during the best
years of his life in dealing with the money of India, to
offer a practical solution to the difficulty : and I appeal
with confidence to the members of this Institute to give
an impartial verdict on the proposal in the interests of
India alone.

APPENDIX.

TABLE ILLUSTRATING THE EFFECT ON THE RESERVES OF THE CURRENCY DEPARTMENT OF THE PROPOSAL TO RECEIVE GOLD IN EXCHANGE FOR SILVER AND NOTES.

Figures show crores of rupees. One crore = Rx. 1,000,000, or at proposed rate £625,000

	Gold Reserve to meet Gold Notes.	Ordinary Reserve of Currency Department.				Total Note Circulation.	Special Gold Reserve to meet New Silver.
		Gold.	Silver.	Securities.*	Total.		
Assumed present position of Currency Department ..	..	..	16	8	24	24	..
Result of 6 crores of gold paid in : 2 for gold notes, 2 for ordinary notes, 2 in exchange for silver	2	4	14	8	26	28	..
8 crores more of gold paid in : 2 for gold notes, 6 in exchange for silver	4	10	8	8	26	30	..
Silver balance having fallen below $+\frac{10 + 8}{2}$ silver is bought and 1 crore coined. The cost is only Rx. 800,000 ; Rx. 200,000 is therefore set aside as the special gold reserve	4	9	9	8	26	30	·2
It is assumed that Rx. 800,000 gold paid for the silver will have been paid in notes, not in actual gold, so that the account will stand thus ..	4	9·8	9	8	26·8	30·8	·2
8 crores more of gold paid in : 2 for gold notes, 2 for ordinary notes, 4 in exchange for silver	6	15·8	5	8	28·8	34·8	·2
Silver balance having fallen below $+\frac{15·8 + 5}{2}$ silver is bought and 4 crores coined,costing Rx.3,200,000 ; Rx. 800,000 is therefore added to special gold reserve. It is assumed that the Rx. 3,200,000 will have been paid in notes and not in gold	6	15·0	9	8	32	38	1

The above Table shows the results of the receipt in three periods of 22 crores in gold ; and of the purchase in two periods of 5 crores of silver.

* [The Securities Reserve of the Currency Department was raised to 10 crores of rupees in December, 1896.]

† Half metallic reserve. See page 42.

THE NEW RUPEE.

(A paper read before the East India Association, on 17th January, 1894.)

THE nature of the important change which took place in the rupee on the 26th of June last, is sometimes mis-understood. It is often forgotten that the change was the result of a determination to adopt a gold standard in India. This is clearly stated in para. 155 of the Com-mittee's report, and again by the Viceroy in his speech at Simla on the passing of the new law. Indeed, the closure of the mints would have been quite unjustifiable except with this end in view. When once, however, the change of standard was determined on, the closure be-came right in principle, and absolutely necessary. It was the first step towards making the rupee a representative of gold. It is inaccurate, however, to describe it, as is sometimes done, as having become a token coin. A token is really—as Mr. Goschen once defined it—a metallic note : an undertaking on the part of the issuer that it shall be generally accepted as the representative of a certain amount of the metallic sub-stance constituting the monetary standard of the country, and that, if necessary, it shall be redeemed in that sub-stance. But the rupee does not fulfil these conditions. Not only is it not yet accepted as representing a certain amount of gold ; not only has no provision yet been promised for its redemption in gold if required ; but even the rate at which it is to be valued in gold has not yet been determined. Neither is it any longer a silver standard coin, for the essence of a metallic standard of valuation is that the substance of which it is composed should be freely convertible into current money.

India has, in fact, now an inconvertible currency differing only from paper in that, besides being more convenient for everyday transactions, it has, in addition to its artificial value (the result of its restricted amount and its position as legal tender money), a certain lesser intrinsic value to back it, while inconvertible paper has frequently nothing behind it but expectations more or less great. There is this further evil too which the present Indian currency shares to some extent with the inconvertible issues of Italy, Russia and Argentina. The amount is at the discretion of the Government, for there is nothing in the law as it at present stands to prevent the Indian Government from indefinitely increasing the amount of its rupee circulation. This is a power which not even the wisest Government should be entrusted with.

The closure of the mints, and the consequent monopoly rupee currency, have to some extent been justified by the result. It was predicted by most of the opponents of the measure that it would cause, not merely a much greater fall in the gold-value of silver than has occurred, but that silver would drag down with it in its fall the gold-value of the rupee. So far, however, from this being the case, notwithstanding a fall of about 15 per cent. in the gold-value of silver, there has been a rise—and a steadiness—in the gold-value of the rupee. But this rise and steadiness have been accompanied by a failure on the part of the Secretary of State to sell his

Council Bills ; a failure which, to say the least of it, has generated great anxiety amongst politicians and men of business of all shades of opinion.

I desire to point out to this Association what in my opinion have been the causes which have prevented this first step towards the introduction of a gold standard into India being attended with a more signal degree of success ; dealing first of all with the mistakes made, as it appears to me, by the Committee, and then with those made by the authorities responsible for Indian finance. And at the risk of being guilty of egoism, I must say that I am not merely wise *after* the event. Some of the faults which have been made, about which there can be no dispute, would not have been made if my advice had been followed.

1. Though the Committee repudiated the intention of closing the mints for the purpose of raising the value of the rupee, the fixing of 1s. 4d. as the rate for the receipt of gold was an admission that they did not object to its being raised from say 1s. 2½d., its then gold-value, to 1s. 4d. It would have been much better, and more consistent with their argument, if a lower *maximum* rate had been fixed : say 1s. 3d. If this had been done the limit would much sooner have been reached, and the rate would much sooner have become effective ; the speculation in rupee paper which occurred on the proposals of the Committee becoming known would have been to a considerable extent avoided : there would not have been that check to the Indian export trade which probably has been caused by the Council trying to force up its bills beyond the market rate of the day : a gradual flow of gold would probably have set in to the East, and the public generally would have had more confidence in the ultimate success of the proposed measure.

2. The old silver standard of value was knocked down
by the closure of the mints without its being stated what
value should be aimed at for the rupee in the new gold
standard which was to be hereafter adopted. Although
for the present 1s. 4d. was the rate above which the
rupee was not to be allowed to rise, it was said that
"circumstances might arise rendering it proper and even
necessary to raise the ratio". One member of the Committee went so far as to indicate that the rupee might
be worked up considerably higher even than the 1s. 6d.
suggested by the Government of India. It had been
determined to take the momentous step of changing the
standard from silver to gold. It should have been determined at the same time at what rate, everything being
considered, this change could with least injustice and
inconvenience be made ; and the determination having
been made it should have been carried out as soon as
possible at whatever sacrifice was necessary. An interval
no doubt must necessarily have occurred between the
announcement of its intentions by the Government and
their absolute fulfilment. But people would have known
the Government intention, and would have gauged the
prospect of its realisation, and appraised the value of
the new currency accordingly.

3. But not only was no attempt made to declare what
the rupee was hereafter to represent in gold : not only
was the basis of all past, present and future contracts to
be left undetermined until it had been proved by experiment up to what figure exchange could be manipulated :
but, almost indeed as a necessary corollary, it was resolved
to try to get a gold standard without any gold at all.
With the exception of Lord Farrer and Sir R. Welby, the
members of the Committee apparently thought it inex-
pedient to attempt to build up a gold reserve. It is

impossible to have a gold standard with an enormous circulation of monopoly rupees unless there is an assurance *that these rupees can be exchanged into gold at the rate fixed. If A sell goods for Rs. 1000 he is not selling them for gold unless he is certain that he can get gold in exchange for rupees if he wants it, and this certainty can never be established unless the Government can undertake always to withdraw in exchange for gold any redundancy of rupee circulation ; and the Government cannot undertake to do this unless it has a reserve of gold. If arrangements had been foreshadowed by which a suitable gold reserve would have been gradually acquired, and if the committee had insisted as a necessary part of the scheme that at all costs, sooner or later, it should be completed by the acquisition of such a reserve as would have enabled the rupee always to remain at the gold par determined, it would have generated confidence and made the attainment of the end easier.

For confidence is the root from which all sound monetary arrangements must spring. The public could hardly be expected to have confidence in the ultimate attainment of a gold standard, the most important features of which —*viz.*, the new gold-value to be assigned to the rupee, and the manner in which its convertibility into gold was to be secured—were left unsettled. And the confidence of the European public was specially necessary for the success of the scheme. With confidence in the new standard of valuation the flow of European capital would tend towards India. With want of confidence it would be just the other way. In the one case the difficulties of the situation would be lightened : in the other they would be increased. Can any one say that the present difficulties are in no degree owing to want of confidence?

4. The first mistake made by the authorities responsible

for Indian finance, after the report of the Committee had
been adopted, was leaving to the discretion of the Government, instead of regulating by law as might easily have
been done, the quantity of rupees to be coined. There is probably no fear of the Government coining too many.   But
the system is bad.   To secure confidence in any currency
system its automatic working should be regulated by law.

5. The next mistake was one made with the best
intentions, but unfortunate in its result.   The action of
the Government of India in not making special provision
for the receipt of bullion bought or contracted for before
26th June did not make friends of the Exchange Banks.

6. The attempt to force up the value of Council Bills
beyond their market value was a fatal mistake.   And here
I may add that a careful perusal of their report will show
that the Committee as a whole were in no way responsible
for this action.   The value of the rupee in gold under the
present monopoly system is simply what can be got for it
in addition to its intrinsic value.   The Committee and the
Viceroy rightly deprecated any forcing up of the gold-
value of the rupee.   It is manifest that any attempt to
force up the gold price of the rupee must operate as a
check on exports from India.   It was certain that the fall
in the gold-value of silver would operate very materially,
at any rate at first, on the exports to silver countries ; and
this made it all the more necessary not to discourage in
any way—nay, rather to encourage—the exports to gold-
using countries.   And yet, though the Secretary of State
had been selling his Council Bills in the early part of
June for 1s. 2⅝d., he yielded to the pressure put on him
from India, and refused to sell them in July, and still
refuses, under 1s. 3¼d.*   There are those who say that if

* [The day after this paper was read it was announced that the
minimum had been removed.]

the normal amount of bills had been sold for what they would fetch, exchange would have gone down to the •bullion point, that is, to below 1s. I do not think so. This appears to be disproved by the maintenance of bank bills all along at a little above 1s. 3d. But even if exchange had fallen to 1s. it would still have been right to have sold the Council Bills. No *dictum* of the Secretary of State can give the rupee a value beyond its market value. We might have been obliged to confess a great disaster, but the disaster, though more prominent, would really have been less than the maintenance of a fictitious rate of exchange by borrowing. There is another point in connection with Council Bills. They are imports * into India. If they cannot be bought at a price which will give the importer a profit, their place will be taken by more profitable imports. From the view of Government the first imports into India should be Council Bills. If it finds that it is being driven out of the market by other imports it must lower its rates. Its very life, at any rate its solvency, depends on its doing so.

It is admitted by every one that one of the principal difficulties in the adoption of the gold standard by India is the amount of silver at present in that country. On 26th June, the Viceroy pledged himself to the adoption of a gold standard. And every ton of silver received in the country after that date made the task more difficult. One of the results of the refusal to sell Council Bills at their market price was the competition of silver as a means of remittance to the East. Since the mints were closed more than Rx. 6,000,000 of silver has been imported into India.† This should have been prevented at all costs.

* [*I.e.*, in settling the trade balance they act in the same way as imports.]

† The net imports of silver into India between 1st July and 31st December, 1893, amounted to Rx. 6,140,000. This, however, includes a

Lord Kimberley said in the House of Lords on 19th December that Sir David Barbour thought the larger part of the recent demand for silver in India was owing to the fall in price inducing the purchase by natives for ornaments. If this be so, and if it continue, one most serious difficulty in the way of introducing a gold standard into India will have disappeared. But if, as seems possible, one cause of the recent absorption of silver by India is that the effects of the change to a gold standard which has been determined on are not yet understood, the sooner means are adopted to make this known the better. Any encouragement which may be given to the poorer classes to look upon silver as still worth its weight in rupees should be jealously watched: any attempt to use their ignorance as a means for bolstering up the price of silver should be firmly opposed. It is understood that a proposal was made by the Government of India to impose an import duty on silver in order to prevent its importation.* I am not prepared to enter on this subject. I will only say that I do not think any advantages to be derived from an import duty are sufficient to counteract its manifest evils. But whether I am right or wrong, the authorities should make up their minds one way or the other at once. The consequences of their remaining so long in "the valley of *indecision*" have already been disastrous. If the importation could not have been stopped by the sale of Council Bills at their market value, it would have been better for the Government to have forced down the price of silver in India by throwing its own spare silver on the market until the price reached such a point that it became unprofitable to ship it from the West. There might have

considerable quantity of silver on its way to India when the mints were closed.
   * [A 5 per cent. duty was shortly after imposed.]

been a serious nominal loss caused by the State breaking
up its rupees, but it would have been only one item in the
necessary cost of the change of standard.

A great deal of mischief has been caused by the mis-
taken action of the past. But it is never too late to
mend. Let those responsible for the Government of
India at once announce that they have determined to
carry out what they have already undertaken, a gold
standard for India. Let there be no more talk of the
possibility of the policy of closing the mints failing. Let
the permanent gold-value aimed at for the rupee be at
once announced and not left to experiment. Let some
scheme be adopted by legislative enactment for gradually
replacing the paper currency reserves with gold, and
gradually accumulating fifteen or twenty millions sterling
of gold, as backing for the Indian currency. Let the
Government announce that at all costs it will persevere in
its undertaking until it finds the rupee for a considerable
time at the *par* determined on, and itself in a position
always to undertake to remove any redundancy by buying
silver rupees at that par with gold. Let it at once admit
the error it has made in the matter of its Council Bills,
and sell them for what it can get for them. Let it stop
shipments of silver to India, if they be not stopped by the
free sale of Council Bills, by melting and selling its own
surplus stock for gold, until the price goes down to the
unprofitable import point, or until it has sufficient gold to
guarantee the new parity of the rupee. Let these general
principles be adopted and considered vital; but let the
details be worked out and secured by legislative enactment
with ample opportunity for examination and discussion.
And I believe the difficulties, if only the rate be not fixed
too high, will gradually disappear.

There are some who think that India cannot have a

gold standard without there being such a further demand
on the gold stock of the world as will still further aggra-
vate the evil of low price, from which we are thought to
be now suffering. I know I am treading on difficult
ground, and perhaps the matter is not a suitable one for
discussion before this Association.   But this much I
venture to say : That gold prices depend on the value of
gold, and not on the quantity of money which may be in
existence at any time.   That the value of gold depends,
like other commodities, not merely on supply and demand
but on the cost of its production.   That much of the
alteration in the relative values of gold and other commodities which has undoubtedly taken place in the past has
been due to the fact that the labour of man, when applied
to the production of other commodities, has increased in
productivity, but when applied to the production of gold,
has not so increased, or at any rate not in the same
degree.   That gold has not yet been influenced so much
by the cheapness of production, which is the main feature
of the past few years, as other commodities have been.
Be this, however, as it may ; the gold required to establish
a gold currency in India is one amount; that required
merely to back and secure the existing rupee currency
must be much smaller.   It is the latter only, and not the
former, which will have to be secured.   When Sir David
Barbour talks of being able to secure the convertibility of
rupees into sovereigns with only £15,000,000 to start with,
and when it is remembered that the annual production of
gold is now £6,000,000 more than it was three years ago,
this should certainly not be an impossible task.

THE INDIAN MONETARY PROBLEM.

(Reprinted from the *Asiatic Quarterly Review*, April, 1894.)

ON the 26th June, 1893, in consequence of the recom-
mendations of a Committee presided over by the Lord
Chancellor of England, an Act was passed at Simla closing
the Indian mints against the free coinage of silver. One
of the most important changes ever made in the monetary
system of a great country was thus commenced. It is
not proposed here to discuss the wisdom of the policy
then inaugurated; or to examine the relative merits of
silver, of gold, and of the two metals together, as a standard of valuation. It is desired rather to draw attention
to the objects aimed at by Lord Herschell's Committee;
to explain the measures taken in the furtherance of those
objects; and to see the results which have followed.

The change was recommended by the Committee, and
adopted by the Government, with the object of eventually
putting the money of India on a gold basis. This was
not only admitted by the Committee in saying "we cannot advise your Lordship to overrule the proposals for the
closing of the mints and the adoption of a gold standard,"
but it was also expressly stated by Lord Lansdowne,
during the discussion on the bill, that "we intend to intro-
duce a gold standard". And indeed otherwise the closure
of the mints, which became necessary directly it was determined to change the standard of valuation, would have

been quite unjustifiable. When therefore "the Indian currency experiment" is talked of, it should be remembered that the closure of the mints was hardly an experimental act. It was the necessary sequence of a deliberate decision to forsake a silver, and to adopt a gold, standard of valuation. Experiment was to decide how the gold standard was to be engrafted on to the money circulation and obligations of the country, and how it was to be maintained.

It is necessary to explain what a gold standard of valuation is. Unfortunately no authoritative definition can be given. An American writer of eminence indeed once gave nine different meanings as attached to the word "standard" when used in monetary discussions. But no one of these meanings is comprehensive enough to indicate the sense in which the word is used in the report of the Committee and the speech of Lord Lansdowne. It may, however, be safely said, that the standard of valuation of a country is the commodity in terms of which, by law and custom, all other commodities are expressed when their money values are stated; and that the commodity selected is only effective as the standard of valuation when it can be changed freely into the current money of the country, and when the current money of the country can be changed freely into it, at the established rate. Thus before the 26th of June, silver was the standard of India; not because rupees, and their fractional copper representatives, constituted the currency of the country, but because whoever chose could turn his silver into the currency of the country, and could equally turn the currency of the country into silver.* So that in effect it

* The seigniorage of 2 per cent. is left out of consideration. Theoretically it interferes with the exactness of the standard: but practically it is not important.

was not how many rupees or pice were given, but how much silver was given, for particular commodities. And a gold standard cannot be attained until gold occupies a similar position. Not until gold can always be turned at a fixed rate into rupees, or their fractional representatives, or into whatever may be the currency of the country, and not until the currency of the country can be exchanged into gold at the same rate, will all the monetary transactions of India really be measured by gold, and will a gold standard be established in that country. The particular way in which a gold standard was to be set up in India was not set forth in the recommendation of the Committee. Indeed, the members were not unanimous on some important matters connected with it. Some apparently thought that it might be possible to maintain a gold standard without gold being provided by the Government. Others, rightly as it seems to me, considered that the Government of India should " accumulate a sufficient reserve of gold ". The rate too at which the rupee should stand in the gold valuation was not settled, the Committee generally, while proposing a major limit of 1s. 4d. for the present, said that " it would not, of course, be essential to the plan that the ratio should never be fixed above 1s. 4d. ; circumstances might arise, rendering it proper, and even necessary, to raise the ratio ".[*] And one member of the Committee clearly indicated his view that a return to the old Latin Union rate of something like 1s. 10½d. the rupee, might eventually be possible.

But in regard to " the closing of the mints against the free coinage of silver " there was no uncertain sound ;

---

[*] What was probably in the mind of the Committee was the possibility of a rise in the gold value of silver (owing to a bimetallic union or other causes) bringing the ratio of silver to gold lower than 21·9 to 1, the ratio corresponding to 1s. 4d. the rupee.

and this momentous preliminary step was in due course
taken ; and silver ceased to be the standard of the country.
Prices in India, being no longer determined by the value*
of the commodity silver, became dependent on the limited
quantity of rupees in circulation.   It was expected that,
this quantity remaining unaltered, the level of rupee
prices at the time of the closure of the mints would
also remain unaltered, and that the value of the rupee
having (owing to its coinage being stopped) been made
greater than the value of the silver contained in it,
its value in gold at the date of the stoppage would at least
be maintained, and would gradually be enhanced. But
many of those who approved of the closure of the
mints were not confident that these expectations would
be realised. It was felt that the quantity of rupees in
circulation might be increased notwithstanding the closure
of the mints, and that prices expressed in the monopoly
rupees of all commodities, including gold, might con-
sequently rise. And so far as can be seen this is precisely what has happened,* though probably the increased
quantity of rupees in circulation has partly arisen from
a cause which was not foreseen. A ceaseless stream of
rupees has been pouring into India, which, but for a
ceaseless outlet into hoards and ornaments, would have
unduly flooded the country.† This stream had been
running with unusual volume during the last two or
three years, and new rupees must have continued to flow

* It is not unreasonable to suppose too that the fall in the price
of silver, which was bound to follow the closure of the mints, has been
to some extent arrested in India by the increased quantity of rupees
in circulation.

† It has been established by the careful researches of Mr. F. C.
Harrison and Professor Edgeworth (see *Economic Journal*, 1891, 1892,
1893) that till lately the volume of rupee *circulation* has remained
practically constant.

over the country for a long time after the mints were closed. But the outlets were practically closed directly the value of silver was divorced from the rupee, thus causing the volume of circulation in the country to increase, and not only hindering any enhancement in the gold value of the coin, but preventing the arrest which the Committee expected would take place in its fall.

And the difficulty has been aggravated by the action of the Home Government to which attention will now be drawn. The Committee recommended that, with the object of preventing any sudden rise in the gold value of rupees, they should be issued in exchange for gold at the rate of 1s. 4d. This arrangement, though unquestionably wise in itself, gave rise to some misunderstanding. Nowhere in the report of the Committee is any expectation held out that this rate would soon be attained. But the public assumed it would not have been named unless there had been confidence that the rupee, which stood at 1s. 4d. in February, 1892, would soon, with the closure of the mints, rise again to that figure. And, immediately it was known that the mints were to be closed with a major limit of 1s. 4d., speculation occurred in rupee paper, which had the effect of working up the exchange rate from about 1s. 2½d. to 1s. 4d. ; and the favourable views were thus confirmed. One eminent English political economist* asked in seriousness whether the Government would "not attempt now to exercise the power which they appear to have contemplated employing, and move the rate of exchange to the position it held till 1872, in which year the average rate obtained for Indian Council Bills was 1s. 11·125d.". Even the Government of India were misled into thinking that a

* Mr. Inglis Palgrave, *Times*, 6th July, 1893.

rate of 1s. 4d. could be maintained, and urged the Secretary of State not to sell his Council Bills at a lower figure. The Secretary of State yielded to the clamour of Calcutta ; • and, though he subsequently reduced the minimum to 1s. 3¼d., it was not until the end of January, nearly seven months after the mints were closed, that he was forced to admit that the gold price of rupees in India was independent of his fiat. Meanwhile Council Bills had not been sold.* The export trade of India, which leans so much on them, and which (as the successful introduction of a gold standard depended entirely on the excess of exports over imports being maintained) needed special encouragement at the time, was disorganised ; the debt owing to England by India was accumulating ; and money was being borrowed in London while funds were lying idle in Calcutta and Bombay. Imports of silver, no longer wanted for money in India, and of which indeed there was a redundancy in the currency and in the Government Treasure Chests, were encouraged—thus giving a stimulus to the price of the metal, not likely to be maintained when things had settled down. Imports of other goods into India were encouraged by the competition of Council Bills being practically withdrawn ;—imports which, however desirable in themselves, were of not such primary importance to the Empire of India as that the State liabilities to England should not be increased.

Before the close of January it was announced that a minimum for the Council Bills would no longer be maintained, and it was soon seen that the market price was considerably below 1s. 2⅝d.,—the price ruling when

* In the last six months of 1893 only 114 lakhs of bills were sold, compared with 1134 lakhs in the corresponding period of the previous year.

the mints were closed. Even at the reduced rates the full amounts offered were not at first taken up; but allowance must be made for the disorganisation which has occurred in consequence of the usual channels of remittance having been altered, and for that mistrust which a vacillating Government policy must always cause.

It is impossible to say at what rate exchange will settle down. There are some who still prophesy that the gold value of the rupee will fall to the intrinsic gold value of the silver contained in it. Experience, up to the present time, indicates that they are wrong. Exchange has to some extent fallen with silver, and this must be so while shipments of silver to India continue. But the large margin between the exchange gold value of the rupee and its intrinsic gold value has varied very little since January, when the Secretary of State began to sell his bills without a minimum.* The rate of exchange must, of course, be subject to much greater fluctuations than if the rupee were on an effective gold basis. It will mainly depend on the rupee prices of commodities in India, and on the gold prices of commodities in places with which she trades; but, as has already been stated, the most important factor in determining rupee prices will be the quantity of rupee currency. If there be no disturbing causes, any redundancy of currency in India will, in process of time, be worked off; prices will gradually fall; and the gold value of the rupee will gradually rise, till it reaches the point at which it will be profitable to import gold.

---

* On the 31st of January, 1894, the melting value of the rupee in London was 11⅜d. against 14⅜d. (the price obtained for Council Bills). On the 7th of March following, it was 10₁₀⁷d. against 14d. [The margin has now largely increased. See diagram at beginning of volume.]

But this result will not be attained if India, on balance
of trade, do not pay what she may owe, whether it be
in the shape of obligations incurred in England or for
goods which she imports. If she become a debtor, instead of, as she has been in the past, a creditor *
country, the exchange value of the rupee must fall,
until it eventually reaches the silver bullion price. It
was this point which was apparently lost sight of
when the Secretary of State ruinously affected the export trade by declining to sell his bills at their market
value.

Again, the transfer of capital from India to England
would also unfavourably affect the position of the former
country ; while the transfer of capital from England to
India would tend in the opposite direction. In this view
it is of the highest importance that the capitalist of the
West, as well as the people of India, should have confidence in the future of Indian money. The value of an
inconvertible paper currency depends to a material extent
on the prospects of its ultimate redemption ; and a similar
remark applies to the value of the inconvertible rupee.
If a definite and attainable scheme be set forward for the
ultimate security of the rupee on a gold basis, it will tend
to confidence in it, and to an increase in its gold value :
and the flow of capital to India will be encouraged.

The first point in this connection is to fix the rate in
gold at which the rupee is eventually to stand. It goes
without saying that the lower this is fixed the sooner, and
with the greater ease, will the gold point be reached.
People interested in India are apt to forget that, though,
in respect to its gold obligations, a high rate of exchange

* The exports of India have, in the past, been sufficient to pay for
her imports and the value of the Council Bills, and still to leave her
creditor for a large amount which has been adjusted by specie remittances.

is for the advantage of the State and therefore of its subjects, the trade of the country is just as well served • by a low as by a high rate, provided there be stability. It will probably be admitted that nothing above a 1s. 4d. rupee can now be thought of. A 1s. 3d. rupee, however, would certainly be much easier, and it would put earlier the date on which India might be expected to join in the scramble for gold. If the probable scruples of Lombard Street could be overcome this would certainly seem to be the better rate of the two.

The next point to be settled is how the gold is to be secured. The object is not to supplant the rupee currency, but merely to put it on a gold basis. All that is needed is, that while on the one hand currency shall be given in exchange for gold, on the other hand gold, not necessarily gold coin but (what Ricardo pointed out, when the resumption of specie payments was under discussion in England in 1816, would be equally effectual) gold in any form, shall be given in exchange for currency. The Paper Currency Department in India affords an excellent medium for the gradual acquisition of gold in exchange for its silver reserves.* Whether any, and if so what, attempt should be made to acquire gold before it comes in obedience to trade demands, need not now be discussed. But until the exchange value of the rupee has for some time remained constant at the rate determined, no attempt should be made to free any gold which may have accumulated. If, by a stroke of a magician's wand, the (say) twenty crores of rupees now held by the Paper Currency Department were changed into £13,333,333, the difficulty would not necessarily be solved. If the rupee remained at its present price, or even at (say) 1s. 3d., while the Paper Cur-

* As to the detailed way in which this can be carried out, see pp. 42 to 44.

rency Department offered to redeem its rupee notes in gold at 1s. 4d., the gold would all be replaced by silver in the course of a few days. But if the rupee gradually· worked itself up to 1s. 4d., and if then, in obedience to trade requirements, gold came to India, and the reserves of the Currency Department gradually changed from silver to gold, it would indicate a very different result.

There has been enough of experiment. Owing to the way in which it has been conducted, the object aimed at by Lord Herschell's Committee seems almost as far off as ever; and judging from the telegrams which have recently come from India insisting on the Secretary of State's ability to fix his own price for his bills, much profit has not been derived from the bitter experience. But the advisers of the India Office seem at last to be realising the position; and if, as apparently was the case, it needed this costly lesson to teach them wisdom, it will not have been entirely thrown away. But let the Government hesitate no longer. Let the announcement already made, as to the introduction of a gold standard into India, be emphatically repeated. Let the manner in which the measure is to be carried out; the gold rate to be adopted; the gold security to be obtained; be definitely determined. Let a pledge be given that this policy shall be carried out without wavering. Let it be remembered that there is not always a royal smooth road to success, but that the path which leads thereto is often difficult. Let it not be expected that the results will certainly be attained in a few weeks or months; but let the Government look forward with patience to the gradual establishment, it may be after the lapse of years, of a perfect system under which all the monetary transactions of India shall be measured in gold. As Sir David Barbour has pointed out, it is wrong to think " that the establishment of a gold standard would be a source of endless

wealth to the Government of India ".   But it is believed
that it will relieve the Government from the harassing
•fluctuations of the past, and that it will, when established
on a satisfactory footing, contribute largely to the trade
prosperity of our magnificent empire, and promote the
general welfare of our Indian fellow-subjects.

THE INDIAN MONETARY PROBLEM.

(Reprinted from the *Asiatic Quarterly Review*, October, 1895.)

EIGHTEEN months ago, after placing before the readers of
this review a brief statement of the Indian Monetary
Problem, I urged that, in order to give full effect to the
decision of Lord Herschell's Committee, the manner in
which gold was to replace silver, which had by the closure
of the mints ceased to be the common measure of value
in India, should be definitely settled, the gold rate to be
adopted for the rupee and the gold security by which that
rate was to be maintained being fixed by legislative enactment. Nothing, however, has yet been done; there has
been a policy of drift; of waiting for something to turn
up; of letting the rupee shake down at a chance monopoly
value though its value must certainly be influenced by the
law regulating the standard. The authorities at the India
Office and in Calcutta, profiting by the bitter experience
of the last half of 1893, have indeed been wise enough to
turn a deaf ear to the Indian Currency Association, which
urged that a Government can by manipulation make its
currency of what value it pleases and that such manipulation is expedient. But though Sir Henry Fowler from
his place in Parliament said last year, that " sooner or
later, perhaps the sooner the better, India must come to
have a gold standard," Sir James Westland, so far from
endorsing this statement, has recently qualified his own

assertion, "that the policy of closing the mints is still the policy of the Government," by adding that "it is possible that we may find some relief in measures taken by or in concert with some of these nations" (America, Germany and England) for the restoration of the value of silver. It is submitted that the further delay which must result from this dallying with bimetallism must be harmful, and that India should, without further hesitation, continue the course, in the direction of a gold standard, on which she has embarked.

If there were any reasonable probability of a bimetallic agreement *at such a ratio as would permanently improve the gold value of the rupee*, there might be some justification for Sir James Westland's expectant attitude. But, until the importance of the ratio as a factor in bimetallism is generally admitted, it cannot be too often repeated, that the ratio is the essence of the whole matter. If there were a bimetallic agreement among the leading nations at some ratio not less favourable to silver than say 23·36 to 1 (which would represent the rupee at 15d. and silver at 40·86d. per oz.), and if, as with a ratio approximating that instanced, it seems probable would be the case, the agreement could practically be maintained for a long term of years, there would be a stable exchange between India and the present gold and silver using countries without further trouble. India would join in the scramble for gold, which would become keener according as the ratio was fixed more favourably to silver,* and she might be trusted to safeguard her own interests as a partner in the new convention. But with a ratio less favourable to

---

* At the ratio of 15½ to 1 for instance, it is believed that silver would be so much overvalued as to lead to India at once changing the bulk of its silver hoards into gold.

silver—with a ratio of say 29·2 to 1, representing the
rupee at one shilling and silver at 32¼d. per oz. (a ratio
more favourable to silver than is warranted by its present
price)—though a stable exchange would probably be
secured it would be at a lower rate than has yet been
reached ; and, independently of other considerations, the
loss to the State by the increased cost of remitting its
sterling obligations would be intensified. It is unnecessary to discuss in detail the prospect of an international
agreement on this all-important subject of the ratio ; but
few well-informed persons will deny that, although we
are assured by the leading advocates of bimetallism in the
United States of America and France that nothing but a
ratio of 16 or 15½ to 1 will satisfy them, any remote
chance there may be of Great Britain and Germany join-
ing in an agreement is confined to a ratio nearly approach-
ing the gold value of silver at the present time. When
then there is so little prospect of agreement, when the
only chance of the consent of two at least of the dominant
partners in the agreement being obtained is a ratio little
if at all more favourable to the rupee than that which
prevails at present, it is difficult to see why India should
wait.

It is often assumed that because the closure of the mints
was followed by a great fall in the gold value of silver, its
effect on general commercial interests was disastrous. I
think that inasmuch as it led to the immediate removal of
an artificial prop, by which the value of silver was being
maintained above its real value, the measure was beneficial.
The prop which kept up the value of silver was not, as
may at first sight have appeared, the demand for Indian
currency. It has been conclusively shown that the demand
for the Indian mints was really for hoards and ornaments
which reached their destination through the Indian cur-

rency.* The closure of the channel by which this demand
was satisfied, and possibly the knowledge that silver was
no longer the real standard metal of the country, have
discouraged its absorption ; but notwithstanding this,
the net imports of silver into India in the year ending
March, 1895, were over 27,000,000 oz.—an amount, though
less than the net imports of the immediately preceding
years, yet in excess of those of 1886-87 and of the previous
average.† The main prop which was removed was the
purely artificial demand for an article not wanted created
by the action of the American legislature. The course
of American politics is so uncertain that it is impossible
to say whether the purchases of silver under the Sherman
Act would have continued until the present time if the

* Mr. F. C. Harrison, working on the figures of the annual rupee
censuses which have been taken since 1876, estimates the increase to the
actual rupee circulation in British India during that period at 13 crores
of rupees, while the net imports of silver amounted to 164 crores.

† The following shows the annual net imports of silver into India
since 1872. It is instructive to see that only in the year 1893-94 [when
the imports were unduly swelled *first* by the anticipated closure of the
mints and *secondly* by the shipments of silver to India encouraged by
the minimum fixed by the Secretary of State as the sale price of Council
Bills] did India absorb as much as 54,000,000 oz., the quantity purchased annually by the United States under the Sherman Act. [The
figures for 1895-96 and 1896-97 have now been added for convenience of
reference.]

NET IMPORTS OF SILVER INTO INDIA.

1872-73 to 1885-86 annual average	22,804,000 oz.
1886-87	26,834,000 ,,
1887-88	34,608,000 ,,
1888-89	34,675,000 ,,
1889-90	41,017,000 ,,
1890-91	53,457,000 ,,
1891-92	32,349,000 ,,
1892-93	45,523,000 ,,
1893-94	54,329,000 ,,
1894-95	27,040,000 ,,
1895-96	27,019,000 ,,
1896-97	25,929,000 ,,

closure of the Indian mints had not precipitated President
Cleveland's action. But under the light of recent events
it can hardly be doubted that if these purchases had gone
on, even a Morgan-Rothschild group could not have
prevented gold going to a premium in the terms of the
currency of the United States—a result which would have
been followed by widespread commercial disaster. The
repeal of the Sherman Act would inevitably have ensued,
and with it there would, I believe, even if the Indian
mints had remained open, have been as great a fall in the
gold value of silver as has actually occurred. If the
closure of the mints did nothing else, it at any rate led
to the prompt stoppage of an unreal demand for silver—
an unreal demand which gave it a fictitious value, and
which, like all other unreal demands, was bound to end
sooner or later in a fall rather than in a rise in the value
of the commodity bolstered up.

And the position of India would have been much
worse than it is now. Whatever evils result from a fall
in, and from the uncertainty of, exchange would have been
intensified. The stability of her standard of valuation
would have been menaced by a mass of silver hoarded in
the State vaults at Washington which was of no use as
currency, and which had been proved to be an inefficient
security for monetary obligations.

The closure of the Indian mints, though unaccom-
panied by any definite announcement or at any rate by any
statutory provision as to what was aimed at in the future,
accompanied in the first instance by mismanagement so
gross as to have brought the Indian Exchequer, according
to the views of responsible statesmen, within the verge of
bankruptcy, has done something towards steadying the
gold value of the rupee. The lowest price it has reached
is 12·4d.—its value on the 23rd of January, 1895; while

the highest price reached, after the influence on the
market caused by the stoppage of the sale of Council
Bills had been removed, was 13·8d., on the 29th of August,
1894—a difference of 1·4d. in the rupee it is true, but
a small difference compared to the differences in the past.*

A strong testimony to the wisdom of the closing of the
Indian mints, so far as India is concerned, is afforded by
that sensitive barometer, the London Stock Exchange.
Before the mints were closed the difference between the
yield to the investor in the sterling and in the rupee
securities of the Government of India was nearly $\frac{3}{4}$ per
cent.; it is now only about $\frac{1}{4}$ per cent. Some part of the
improvement in the value of the rupee securities is due to
the fact that they are now guaranteed against repayment
before the expiration of ten years, whereas the old rupee
loans were repayable at three months' notice: but even
allowing for this, it must be admitted that the monopoly
rupee has proved itself to be on the London Stock Exchange a better basis for security than the free silver
coin. What will be the view when the Government has
absolutely pledged itself by legislative enactment to place
the rupee on a gold basis?

Though stability between English and Indian money
will not be reached until exchange can be adjusted by the
remittance of a precious metal which is the common
measure of value in the two countries, the nearer the
prospect there is of such a state of things arising, the
greater will be the stability. And if a reasonable plan for
putting the money of India on a gold basis were announced, a plan which could be carried out by ordinary
commercial action, and which were made independent of

* [There has since been a gradual rise in the gold price of the rupee,
which stood last January, while the Council was still selling bills freely, at
over 15d.]

the volition of Government, it would very materially help
to secure its fulfilment.

The most important point for settlement—the point*
on which the success of any measure for placing Indian
money on a gold basis must depend—is the gold value to
be assigned to the unit of account called the rupee by
which all transactions have been in the past, are now, and
will continue to be, reckoned.   No forecast as to its value
can be made until it is known how much gold the rupee
is to represent.   Just as when arrangements were made
for resuming specie payments in England in 1816 it was
necessary absolutely to fix the weight and fineness of
sovereigns which bank notes were to represent, so it is
necessary now to absolutely determine the weight and
fineness of gold to be indicated by the rupee.   It will be
remembered that, on the recommendation of Lord Herschell's Committee, a major gold limit of 1s. 4d. was adopted
for the rupee.   This was, however, avowedly only a
temporary rate, and it was fixed by the Executive Government, and not by statute.   Although it is to be regretted
that Lord Herschell's Committee did not assume the
responsibility of making a permanent recommendation on
this important subject, their action (as the major temporary limit has never been reached) may be attended with
the undoubted advantage that the final proposals of the
Government will receive full discussion and criticism
before they become law.   The gold value of the rupee
should not be fixed too high.   The lower it is placed the
easier will it be for the parity, between the rupee unit and
the gold which it represents, to be secured ; the nearer
the existing rate it is the less will prices and trade be
disturbed ; the smaller the necessary excess of the nominal
over the intrinsic value of the token the less danger of
fraudulent imitation ; the smaller the difference between

the nominal value of the rupee and the market value of the silver contained in it the less will the holders of the uncoined silver in India (weighing perhaps 350 crores of rupees) appear to suffer by the change. Nearly three years ago, before the mints were closed, I advocated that, in changing the standard of India from silver to gold, the rupee should be taken as representing fifteen pennyworth of gold,* and, though at the time I was severely criticised by some for suggesting a remedy which, it was said, would, even if successful, be no remedy at all, yet so far as can be judged from what has occurred since the closure of the mints, this rate did not err in being too low. Whether, if this rate had been adopted as a permanent basis, and if a plan had been prescribed by law which might have rendered a settlement on this basis possible by the ordinary operations of trade, the rupee would by this time have risen to the suggested gold value, it is not possible to say. But it is certain that the process was hindered by the attempt to force a rate on the market, and by the absence of any definite scheme, or even of any definite policy on this subject.

And this brings us to the consideration of the very important point as to how the attainment and maintenance of the gold parity—let us say 1s. 3d.—are to be secured. Some people are still foolish enough to think that the Secretary of State by the mere announcement of a parity and his determination not to sell bills below it can fix the gold value of the rupee. They are not worth arguing with. But there are others who would be satisfied with the approach to parity which might perhaps be secured by manipulating the quantity of rupee currency. This would, however, be open to many grave objections. If India is

* [See page 40.]

6

to have a gold standard let it be one, not merely in name, but in deed and in truth. There appear to be only two practical ways of securing this. *First:* The gradual introduction of a gold currency suitable to the people of India and the supersession by it of a certain portion of the existing rupee currency. *Second:* The maintenance of the established parity for the existing rupee currency by arrangements for converting what may not be required for purposes of circulation at that parity, into the standard commodity, gold ; and similarly for converting the standard commodity, gold, into silver rupee currency. Sir David Barbour advocates the first course, and it would certainly be the best if there were no question of expense, if there were no doubt as to the sufficiency of the stock of gold in the world, and if it were certain that gold coins would remain in circulation at the parity selected. But it has never been shown that the second course would not effectively maintain the gold value of the silver rupee. It would require less gold ; it would adapt itself more readily to the gradual change ; and the introduction of a gold currency, if this were eventually determined on, would be facilitated by the gradual accumulation of gold in support of the existing rupee currency and by the maintenance of the gold parity which would result from an accumulation of gold sufficient to secure the convertibility of redundant rupees.

Some plan, then, should be settled by law for the gradual acquisition of a gold reserve. Undoubtedly the best, if not the only practical, basis for the operation must be the Indian Paper Currency Department, whose stores of silver, which are as useless with a gold standard as the silver at Washington, should be gradually changed to gold. And as far as possible the conditions under which that gold should be made available for securing the note

issues of the Government, and at the same time for up-
holding the gold value of the rupee currency, should be
now fixed—as little discretion as need be being given to
the Executive.

An obvious plan for securing this is for the Paper
Currency Department to accept gold at the rate determined as part of its metallic reserve, and not to re-issue
it until such time as the gold rate shall be permanently
maintained. The amount of rupee coinage might also be
made to depend, instead of as it does at present on the
action of the Government,* on the relative proportions of
gold and silver in the metallic reserve of the Paper
Currency Department. The law would, of course, be
inoperative, and no gold would come in to the Currency
Department at all, and there would be no increase to the
rupee coinage until the exchange value of the rupee had
reached 1s. 3d., but it is none the less necessary that the
prospective arrangements should now be authoritatively
settled; and their authoritative settlement would, it is
believed, assist in gradually raising the value of the rupee
to the required level. It is very difficult to say how the
gold value of the rupee is now determined. Opinions
differ as to the manner in which the precious metals, with
free open mints, operate as common measures of value.
But all will admit, that with mints closed and with
coinage a monopoly of the Government, the quantity of
coins in circulation is a most important factor in regulating their value. And the gold value of the monopoly
rupee must, therefore, largely depend on the quantity in

* It is quite unlikely that anything of the sort will happen; but as the
law at present stands [see Indian Coinage Act, pp. 96-102] the Government
has the power to coin rupees on its own account, netting the difference
between their intrinsic and market value, and thus depreciating the value
of its monopoly coins. This is, to use Sir James Westland's words,
"opposed to the simplest canons of currency".

circulation. The value of gold itself—in terms of commodities generally—is another factor of equal importance. Until, therefore, there is either a diminution in the quantity of rupees circulating compared with the wants of the community, resulting in a fall in rupee prices and an increase in the purchasing power of the monopoly rupee; or until there is a fall in the value of gold in terms of commodities generally and a decrease in the purchasing power of gold, there will be no very material change in the gold value of the monopoly rupee. Though there are indications that the coined rupees in circulation are in excess of the requirements of the country for exchange transactions at the prices which were in force when the mints were closed,* it would be undesirable to attempt to raise the purchasing power of the rupee by withdrawing any from circulation. But if, as there are also strong indications, there is a gradual decrease in the purchasing power of gold generally and a gradual rise in gold prices, it must act on the gold value of commodities in India, and thus, gradually, on the value of the monopoly rupee, without causing any disturbance of trade or hardship to the people of India. And this seems to be the solution of the difficulty which is at once most desirable and most probable.

There are two other factors on which the gold value of the rupee may depend, to which it is right to allude. The gold value of the rupee can of course never fall below the intrinsic gold value of the silver contained in it. But notwithstanding the prophecies which were freely made before the closure of the mints, that the rupee could not be maintained above its bullion value, even in India where

* Mr. F. C. Harrison, in his review of the last rupee census, estimates that since the mints were closed there has been an expansion of the circulation to the extent of three crores. [Expansion of the circulation has now apparently ceased.]

a 5 per cent. import duty has protected silver, the rupee
has always since the closure of the mints been worth at
least 10 per cent. more than the bullion of which it was
composed. There is a connection between the market
price of silver and the value of the rupee; but it is a connection between its price as an ordinary commodity and
not as the metal of which the money of the country
happens to be made. This factor, then, has not hitherto
operated. But whether, with the rise in gold prices
which has already occurred, and which will, it is believed,
influence silver like any other commodity, it may not
operate later on, it is impossible to predict.

The other factor to which reference has been made is
the prospect of the rupee ultimately acquiring an increased
gold value owing to the operation of any or all of the foregoing causes. But to give full play to this factor—to
enable it to operate apart from speculation—it is necessary
that the intentions of the State regarding the future of
the rupee should be definitely announced and made sure
by legislative enactment.

Mr. Herbert Spencer has been bold enough to suggest
that it is not the duty of the State to interfere in any way
with the currency of a country, but that it should be left
to individual discretion. But it seems to me certain that if
there is one thing more than another in which State intervention is necessary, it is the authoritative declaration of
the commodity which shall ordinarily be the basis of
monetary contracts, and in terms of which exchanges,
unless otherwise specially provided for, are to be carried
out; and it is the duty of the State to see that the interests
of the community at large, and especially of those who, by
their position, are least able to look after their own, are
safeguarded in this important particular.

With the best possible intentions on the part of those

responsible for the Government of India, the interests of
the community have not hitherto been protected in this
matter. Years ago, when the action of Germany, the States
comprising the Latin Union, and the United States of
America showed that, in their opinion at least, silver could
no longer be relied on as the standard of value, India should
have followed suit instead of being allowed to become the
dumping ground for the silver of the world. In the mere
matter of exchanging, by means of their silver rupee
money, the commodities of India for those of other
countries, our Indian fellow-subjects have no doubt been
able to hold their own ; but when they have taken, as they
have done very largely, the commodity silver in adjustment
of the balance due to them ; taken it not like a perishable
article for consumption, but as a store of value ; they have
unwittingly been worsted : for they have taken a commodity which in the markets of the world is relatively
much less valuable than the commodity gold, which they
might, if they had been far-seeing enough, have taken in
its place.* And the community generally has suffered by
the increased cost at which the sterling obligations of the
State have had to be remitted. It is easy, however, to be
wise after the event ; and probably no one of those who,
twenty or thirty years ago, advocated the introduction of
a gold standard into India, understood the real facts of
the case. But there is no room now for further hesitation.
It is the duty of her Majesty's Government to go on with
the scheme which, after careful inquiry, was recommended
by a Committee, composed of experts of different shades of
opinion, but several of whom, it may be remarked, had
by their previous utterances showed that they were
opposed to the action which they felt themselves com-

* [See above, page 5.]

pelled to recommend. It is their duty to do this with sole
regard to the interests of India : unmindful of the wishes
of any section of their supporters, but taking as their key-
note the duty to India so forcibly expressed by Sir Henry
Fowler when he said that every member of the House of
Commons is a member for India.

THE PRESENT INDIAN FAMINE AND THE RUPEE (1896).

(Reprinted from the *Asiatic Quarterly Review*, December, 1896.)

EVERY one must admit the present unsatisfactory condition of the Indian monetary system. When the mints were closed in June, 1893, the silver standard of valuation was destroyed, and its place has been taken by a system of monopoly coins, introduced—as I have already pointed out in this review*—as the first step towards a gold standard of valuation, but continued without any definitely announced policy or aim, in the expectation of something turning up in the chapter of accidents to indicate what should be the next move.

I purpose in the present paper to discuss how the ability of the people and the Government of India to deal with the famine which is now threatened is likely to be affected by the present position of the rupee.

To appreciate the situation it must be understood that though there is a *nexus* between the gold values of silver and of the rupee (as indeed there is between the gold values of any other commodity which India imports and of the rupee), the gold value of silver is no longer the dominant factor in determining the gold value of the

---

* [See "Indian Monetary Problem," April, 1894, and October, 1895, pp. 63-87.]

rupee. As Mr. O'Conor in his review of the trade of India for 1895-96 puts it :—

"The closure of the mints did materially alter the relative positions of the rupee and silver," and " whereas before that date the price of silver obviously determined the sterling value of the rupee it would seem that since that date the value of the rupee is determined by quite other factors ".

The most prominent result of this divergence of value between silver and the rupee is the way in which it affects the hoards of that metal held as ornaments or in other un-coined form by the people of India. It is calculated that such hoards amount to 1,312,500,000 ounces, representing under the old value Rx. 350,000,000, but now, with silver quoted in India at Rs. 79¾ per 100 tolas (it has been as low as Rs. 79¼), worth only Rx. 255,870,000.* And it must be remembered that these hoards are not held merely by the wealthy. The peasants have for long been accus-tomed to use this form for their savings ; and in times of pressure have raised money, either by loan or by sale, on these hoards, realising probably the value in rupees corre-sponding to their weight. But now all this is changed, and though I am told there is no cause for political anxiety on this account it must appear hard to the people that their silver should be worth 94 crores of rupees less than it was formerly. Whether it is the silver which has fallen in value or the rupee which has risen in value need not be discussed. In the case of all commodities other than silver any alteration in price would have been naturally ascribed to the cheapness (or dearness) of the commodity itself, the dearness (or cheapness) of the rupee not being thought of by practical people. But in the case of silver —accustomed as the people of India have been for so long to look on their silver as rupees in another form—I cannot

* Silver is quoted in India 100 tolas of fine silver. The London quotation is for silver ⅔⅔ fine. The rupee is ⅓⅓ fine.

think that they will look on the alteration in relative value as an ordinary incident of trade. I fear they may be induced to believe they have not been dealt fairly with in this effect of the change of the standard of valuation which has taken place. Should, however, happily my fears be groundless, and should the pesent relation of the monopoly rupee to uncoined silver be accepted without demur, it seems to me that the Government and the people of India are in a better position to deal with the famine under the present system than they would have been had the mints remained open for the coinage of silver. For the loss which holders of uncoined silver have appeared to suffer is compensated by the increased purchasing power which its monopoly character has given to the rupee. Whatever doubts may exist as to the manner in which gold and silver operate as measures of value—whether, as some think, the quantity circulating as money determines prices, or whether, as seems more probable, the quantity of money in circulation in countries with open mints is the result rather than the cause of the relative values of the standard metals and other commodities—it will be generally admitted that where the quantity of money is effectively limited by the action of the State such limitation must materially operate in reducing prices. And this process must be now going on in India, though owing to the peculiar circumstances of the country it can only be traced with difficulty. The extension of railways is operating as a great leveller * of prices, and by raising them in some places and lowering them in others is causing ordinary statistics to be misleading; and no scheme

* This is strikingly illustrated by the following extract from a telegram from the Viceroy in the beginning of November: " Effect of railways will be apparently to diffuse distress, making it more general, but less intense ".

has yet been devised for separating alterations due to good or bad harvests from those which result from other causes. If the mints had remained open rupee prices of food produced in the country would have been higher than they are at present, and the peasantry, though they may not see it, have gained at least as much by the decreased rise in the price of their food as they have lost by the apparent decreased value of their silver ornaments.

Any calculation as to what the gold price of silver would have been if the Indian mints had not been closed, must be more or less speculative. Sentiment may have something to say to it, but the relative values of gold and silver,* as the relative values of other commodities, must be determined by supply and demand and cost of production. Although the suspension of the purchase of 54,000,000 ounces of silver per annum by the United States Treasury under the Sherman Act was precipitated by the closure of the Indian mints, recent events have shown that it would have occurred, though perhaps a few months later, even if they had remained open. This demand for silver, which was a most powerful factor in keeping up its gold value, was not therefore dependent on the Indian mints remaining open. And even the Indian demand has been much less influenced by the closure of the mints than was generally anticipated. The net imports in 1895-96 amounted to 27,018,000 ounces, which was more than the imports of 1886-87,† and considerably above the average of the years 1872-73 to 1885-86. It seems probable that if the mints had remained open the London gold price of silver, though perhaps it might not have touched 2s. 3d., the lowest point to which it has

* Without entering into the question of bimetallism I assume that at present it is out of the range of practical politics.

† [For figures of intervening years see page 77.]

actually fallen, would at any rate have fallen low enough
to bring the value of the rupee nearly down to the shilling
which was almost reached in the beginning of 1895. And
the diversions in value would have been greater than
have actually occurred. The air would have been fuller
of rumours caused by the uncertainty of both the American and Indian situations; and though there might not
have been the great slump in the value of silver which
occurred in June, 1893, and which continued with but
little interruption till March, 1894, there would have been
more frequent and greater movements both down and up
from which the great fall has saved us. I believe that on
the whole the rupee has had not merely a higher, but also
a steadier, gold value, than it would have had if by the
mints being kept open it had been allowed to follow the
course of silver.

Now let us see what effect this tendency of the gold
value of the rupee to rise and to become more steady has
on the ability of the Government and people of India to
cope with the famine which is now threatened.

First of all the rising exchange must encourage imports
into India. The rupee, being able to buy more gold, will
be able to buy more commodities priced in gold. This
process of course will not go on for ever. In commerce
between two countries commodities are really exchanged
for each other and not for the money (gold or silver or
paper or monopoly coins) in terms of which the exchanges
of the commodities are so to speak registered. And
sooner or later the proper adjustment will take place in
the local prices of the commodities themselves, even
though it may be the case of Californian wheat measured
in gold dollars on the one hand and Indian tea measured
in monopoly rupees on the other. But just at first while
the change in the relative values of the two recording

media is taking place—while there is, to use an expression of Mr. Leonard Courtney, " a temporary hardening of the conditions here and a temporarily increased facility of conditions elsewhere "—there will be an encouragement to export from the country the value of the money of which is relatively falling. Just as it was urged that the falling exchange encouraged exports from India so now the rising exchange will temporarily tend to encourage exports from gold using countries.

But let us take a wider view. What effect will the altered position of the rupee have on Indian trade generally ?

As I have said before—as cannot be too strongly insisted upon—it is not a high, nor a low, but it is a stable rate of exchange which is required in the interests of Indian trade. The unautomatic condition of the currency constitutes a serious danger to Indian trade. But I believe that this difficulty might be met if the Government acted with wisdom and courage. Those who have noted what I have written and said on this subject will remember that before the mints were closed I advocated 1s. 3d. as the permanent rate at which gold should be received in exchange for rupees.* It is undeniable that if this rate had been permanently adopted the currency of India would have already been automatically replenished by means of gold paid into the Treasury and held as part of the currency reserve in exchange for rupees which would have been added to the circulation. There would then have been for all practical purposes a gold standard of valuation in India at the rate of 1s. 3d. to the rupee. If at that valuation the currency proved insufficient for the work it had to do, it would have auto-

* [See p. 40.]

matically expanded, and there would have been no talk, as
unfortunately there is now, of a possible financial crisis
owing to a deficiency of the circulating medium. Even •
now Lombard Street is waking to the possibility of the
shipment of gold at the higher rate of 1s. 4d., and if this
rate * be reached without financial trouble, it will result
in the necessary expansion of the currency, and any
danger there may be owing to trade suffering from in-
sufficiency of the circulating medium will be removed.
Exports will then be found to pay for the food grains
imported, and just as India has in the past out of her
abundance met the wants of the West, so the West out
of her plenty will succour India in the time of her need.
What is wanted is only that the currency should be
adequate to the requirements of trade, and that there
should be some assurance as to the position on which it
is to be permanently placed.   The measure of value
should be such that it cannot be tampered with.   The
State may indeed have to borrow to meet its expenditure
on famine relief and its deficient land revenue, but lenders
will be readily forthcoming if they are assured as to the
character of the money in which their principal and
interest will be paid. A 1s. 3d. rupee would have lightened
the task of Government, and would have been better for
many reasons, but a 1s. 4d. rupee is probably not impossible.†
    The Indian legislature will shortly have under its

---

* The rate will really have to be a little more than 1s. 4d. to cover
cost of freight, insurance, etc.

† A plan by which the Indian currency could be made automatic was
explained in the form of a draft bill to amend the Indian Coinage and
Currency Acts published in the *Bankers' Magazine* for April, 1896. [See
p. 113.] It formulated a scheme under which gold sent to India could,
until the rupees it represented were actually required for circulation in the
provinces, be specially ear-marked, and thus, while temporarily strengthen-
ing the money market in the large banking centres, be available for return
to Europe should the necessity for retaining it in India pass away.

consideration a scheme for increasing the rupee circulation by releasing two crores from the cash reserve of the Paper
• Currency Department. This measure is probably under existing circumstances advisable, though it will tend to retard the acquisition of gold at the prescribed rate. But let it be remembered that the object of the Government should be, not any temporary alleviation of monetary pressure, but the placing of the currency of India on a wholesome footing under which its amount shall be automatically regulated without State intervention. There is food enough in the world and to spare. Its distribution can be best undertaken by the ordinary operations of trade. Let the State see that these are not hindered by the absence of sound money.

P.S.—An Act increasing the Paper Currency Department investment by two crores of rupees was passed through all its stages yesterday in Calcutta with the express object of relieving the money market. This emphasises what I have said as to the necessity for putting the currency of India on such a footing that it shall be independent of State interference.

18th December, 1896.

ACT No. XXIII. OF 1870.

An Act to consolidate and amend the law relating to Coinage and the Mint.

[As modified up to date.]

Preamble. WHEREAS it is expedient to consolidate and amend the law relating to Coinage and the Mint : It is hereby enacted as follows :—

I. PRELIMINARY.

Short title. 1. This Act may be called "The Indian Coinage Act, 1870".

2. [*Repeal of enactments.*] *Repealed by Act XII. of* 1873.

Interpretation clause. 3. In this Act, the expression "mint" includes the mints at Calcutta, at Bombay, and at such other places (if any) as the Governor-General in Council, by notification in the *Gazette* of India, from time to time directs ;

The expression "mint rules" means such rules as the Governor-General in Council from time to time prescribes for the management of the mint ;

And the expression "remedy" means variation from the standard weight and fineness.

II. GOLD COINAGE.

Gold coins. 4. The under-mentioned gold coins only shall be coined at the mint :—

(1) A gold mohur or fifteen-rupee piece ;

(2) A five-rupee piece equal to a third of a gold mohur ;

(3) A ten-rupee piece equal to two-thirds of a gold mohur ;

(4) A thirty-rupee piece or a double gold mohur.

5. The standard weight of the said gold mohur shall _{Their stan-} be one hundred and eighty grains troy, and its standard _{dard weight and fineness} fineness shall be as follows : Eleven-twelfths or one hundred and sixty-five grains of fine gold, and one-twelfth or fifteen grains of alloy.

The other gold coins shall be of proportionate weight and of the same fineness :

Provided that, in the making of gold coins, a remedy _{Remedy allowed.} shall be allowed of an amount not exceeding two-thousandths in weight and two-thousandths in fineness.

III. Silver Coinage.

6. The under-mentioned silver coins only shall be _{Silver coins.} coined at the mint :—

(1) A rupee to be called the Government rupee ;

(2) A half-rupee ;

(3) A quarter-rupee, or four-anna piece ;

(4) An eighth of a rupee, or two-anna piece.

7. The standard weight of the Government rupee shall _{Their stan-} be one hundred and eighty grains troy, and its standard _{dard weight and fineness} fineness shall be as follows : Eleven-twelfths or one hundred and sixty-five grains of fine silver, and one-twelfth or fifteen grains of alloy.

The other silver coins shall be of proportionate weight and of the same fineness :

Provided that, in the making of silver coins, a remedy _{Remedy allowed.}

shall be allowed of an amount not exceeding the following :—

	Remedy in weight.	Remedy in fineness.
Rupee . . . ·⎫ Half-rupee . . ⎬ Quarter-rupee . . ⎭ Eighth of a rupee . .	Five-thousandths Seven-thousandths ⎫ Ten-thousandths ⎭	Two-thousandths. Three-thousandths.

IV. COPPER COINAGE.

Copper coins.　8. The under-mentioned copper coins only shall be coined at the mint :—

    (1) A double pice, or half-anna ;
    (2) A pice, or quarter-anna ;
    (3) A half-pice, or one-eighth of an anna.
    (4) A pie, being one-third of a pice, or one-twelfth of an anna.

Their weight.　9. The weight of the double pice shall be two hundred grains Troy.

    The other copper coins shall be of proportionate weight :

Remedy allowed.　Provided that, in the making of copper coins, a remedy shall be allowed of an amount not exceeding one-fortieth in weight.

V. DEVICES ON COINS.

Present devices on coins.　10. Until the Governor-General in Council otherwise orders under the power hereinafter conferred, the coins coined under this Act shall bear on the obverse the likeness of Her Majesty Queen Victoria, and the inscription "Victoria Queen," and on the reverse the designation of the coins in English filled by the word "India," with such date and embellishments on each coin as the Governor-General in Council from time to time determines.

11. The Governor-General in Council may, from time Power to to time, by notification in the *Gazette* of India, direct the order other devices. coining and issuing of all coins authorised by this Act, and prescribe, in lieu of the likeness and inscription here-inbefore mentioned, such other likeness and inscription for all or any of the said coins as he thinks fit.

VI. LEGAL TENDER.

12. No gold coin shall be a legal tender in payment Gold coin not a legal or on account. tender.

13. The said rupee and half-rupee shall be a legal Rupees and half-rupees ɛ tender in payment or on account : legal tender.

Provided that the coin has not lost more than two per cent. in weight :

Provided also that it has not been clipped or filed, or defaced or diminished, otherwise than by use.

The quarter-rupee and eighth of a rupee shall be legal Four-anna and two-ann tender only for the fractions of a rupee, subject to the pieces. second proviso contained in this section.

14. The double pice shall be a legal tender for the Copper coin when a thirty-second part of a rupee or for half an anna ; legal tender

The pice for the sixty-fourth part of a rupee or for one-fourth of an anna ;

The half-pice for the one hundred and twenty-eighth part of a rupee or for one-eighth of an anna ;

And the pie for the hundred and ninety-second part of a rupee or for one-twelfth of an anna :

Provided that none of the said copper coins shall be a legal tender, except for the fractions of a rupee.

15. All silver coin of the weight and standard specified Coin made under form in the Acts No. XVII. of 1835, No. XXI. of 1838, and No. Acts. XIII. of 1862, issued since the passing of those Acts, respectively, and declared by those Acts, respectively, to be a legal tender,

And all copper coins of the weight specified in Acts No. XXI. of 1835, No. XXII. of 1844 and No. XIII. of 1862, issued since the passing of those Acts, respectively, and declared by those Acts, respectively, to be a legal tender,

Shall continue to be a legal tender for the amounts thereof, respectively, subject to the same conditions and provisions as under those Acts, respectively, anything contained in this Act or in any Act hereby repealed not-withstanding.

VII. DIMINISHED, COUNTERFEIT AND CALLED-IN COIN.

Cutting certain silver coins.   16. When any silver coin purporting to be coined and issued under the authority of the Government of India is tendered to any officer authorised by the Governor-General in Council or the Local Government to act under this section, who has reason to believe it to have lost, by reasonable wearing, more than two per cent. in weight,

> Or to be counterfeit,
> Or to have been reduced in weight otherwise than by reasonable wearing,
> Or to be called in by any proclamation,
> He may, by himself or another (subject to the rules which the Governor-General in Council prescribes in this behalf),
> Cut or break such coin.

Return of cut coin.   17. If any coin so cut or broken is counterfeit, or has been reduced in weight otherwise than by reasonable wearing, the pieces shall be returned to the person tendering the coin, and he shall bear the loss caused by such cutting or breaking.

Receipt of cut coin.   But if it has been coined and issued by the authority of the Government of India, and has lost, by reasonable

wearing, more than two per cent. in weight, or has been
called in by any proclamation, the officer cutting or
breaking the same shall receive it at the rate of one rupee
per tola.

18. No suit or other proceeding shall be maintained ^{Bar of suits}
against any person in respect of anything done by him ^{for acts done bond fide.}
bond fide pursuant to this Act.

VIII. COINAGE OF BULLION.

19 to 26. [*Repealed by Act VIII. of* 1893.]

IX. POWER TO MAKE RULES.

27. The Governor-General in Council may, from time ^{Rules as to officers and management of the mint.}
to time—

(1) Fix the number and duties of the officers of, and
persons employed in, the mint ;

(2) Make rules and give directions (subject to the
provisions of this Act and any notification
made thereunder) respecting the management
of the mint, and revoke and alter such rules
and directions.

28. The Governor-General in Council may also, from ^{Rules by notification.}
time to time, by notification in the *Gazette* of India—

(1) Diminish the amount of remedy allowed by
sections 5, 7 and 9 in the case of any coin ;

(2) Determine in the case of any coin the date and
embellishments to be put thereon ;

(3) Call in coins of any date or denomination, or any
coins coined before the date in the notification
mentioned ;

(4) Prescribe rules for the guidance of officers
authorised to cut or break coin under section
16 :

(5) Prescribe the charge to be made on account of the loss and expense of refining ;

(6) Determine the period for which certificates granted under section 24 shall run ;

(7) Fix the fee payable under section 25 ;

(8) Establish a mint at any place in British India, other than Calcutta and Bombay ;

(9) Abolish any mint so established or any mint now existing in British India ;

(10) Regulate any matters relative to coinage and to the mint, which are not provided for by this Act ;

(11) Revoke or alter any notification previously made under this Act.

Every such notification shall come into force on the day therein in that behalf mentioned, and shall have effect as if it were enacted in this Act.

ACT No. XX. OF 1882.

An Act to amend the law relating to the Government Paper Currency.

[As modified up to date.]

Preamble. WHEREAS it is expedient to amend the law relating to the Government Paper Currency : It is hereby en-acted as follows :—

I. PRELIMINARY.

Short title.   1. This Act may be called " The Indian Paper Currency Act, 1882 ".

Local extent.   It extends to the whole of British India ;

Commence-ment.   And it shall come into force on the passing thereof.

2. (1) Act No. III. of 1871 (*to consolidate and* amend *the law relating to the Government Paper Currency*) is hereby repealed. Act No. III. of 1871 repealed.

(2) All appointments made, rules prescribed, notifications published, authorities conferred, securities purchased and notes issued under the said Act, or any Act thereby repealed, shall, if in force, undisposed of or in circulation when this Act comes into force, be deemed to be respectively made, prescribed, published, conferred, purchased and issued under this Act. And all references made to any portion of the Indian Paper Currency Act, 1871 (III. of 1871), or any Act thereby repealed, in Acts or Regulations passed before this Act comes into force, shall be deemed to be made to the corresponding portion of this Act.

II. THE DEPARTMENT OF PAPER CURRENCY.

3. (1) There shall continue to be a Department of the public service, whose function shall be the issue of promissory notes of the Government of India, payable to bearer on demand, for such sums, not being less than five rupees, as the Governor-General in Council from time to time directs. Department of Paper Currency.

(2) Such notes shall be called currency notes.

(3) The Department shall be called the Department of Paper Currency.

4. At the head of the Department there shall be an officer called the Head Commissioner of Paper Currency, and there shall be three other officers, called respectively, the Commissioner of Paper Currency for Madras, the Commissioner of Paper Currency for Bombay, and the Commissioner of Paper Currency for Rangoon. Head Commissioner. Commissioners for Madras, Bombay and Rangoon.

5. The Governor-General in Council may, from time to time, by order notified in the *Gazette* of India— Power to establish Circles of Issue, etc.

(a) Establish districts, to be called Circles of Issue, four of which circles shall include the towns of Calcutta, Madras, Bombay and Rangoon, respectively ;

(b) Appoint in each circle some one town to be the place of issue of currency notes, as hereinafter provided ;

(c) Establish in each such town an office or offices of issue ;

(d) Establish in any town situate in any circle an office, to be called a Currency Agency ; and

(e) Declare that, for the purposes of this Act, any town, other than Calcutta, Madras, Bombay or any town situate in British Burma, in which an office of issue is established, shall be deemed to be situate within such Presidency as is specified in the order.

Deputy Commissioners and Currency Agents.
6. For each Circle of Issue, other than those which include the towns of Calcutta, Madras, Bombay and Rangoon, there shall be an officer called the Deputy Commissioner of Paper Currency, and for each Currency Agency an officer called the Currency Agent.

Subordination of Commissioners, etc.
7. For the purposes of this Act,

(a) The Commissioners of Paper Currency for Madras, Bombay and Rangoon, and the Deputy Commissioners of Paper Currency in the Presidency of Fort William in Bengal, shall be subordinate to the Head Commissioner of Paper Currency ; and

(b) The Deputy Commissioners of Paper Currency in the Presidencies of Fort St. George and Bombay and in the Province of British Burma, shall be subordinate to the Commissioners of Paper

Currency for Madras, Bombay and Rangoon, respectively;

(c) The Currency Agent at any town shall be subordinate to the Head Commissioner, Commissioner, or Deputy Commissioner, as the case may be, of Paper Currency for the Circle of Issue in which that town is situate.

8. All officers under this Act shall be appointed and may be suspended or removed by the Governor-General in Council.

<small>Appointment, suspension and removal of officers.</small>

III. Supply and Issue of Currency Notes.

9. (1) The Head Commissioner shall provide currency notes of the denominations prescribed under this Act, and shall supply the Commissioners and the Currency Agents subordinate to him, and the Deputy Commissioners, with such notes as they need for the purposes of this Act.

<small>Head Commissioner to provide and distribute currency notes.</small>

(2) The Commissioners and Deputy Commissioners shall supply the Currency Agents subordinate to them, respectively, with such notes as those agents need for the purposes of this Act.

(3) Every such note shall bear upon it the name of the town from which it is issued.

10. (1) The name of the Head Commissioner, of one of the Commissioners, of a Deputy Commissioner or of some other person authorised by the Head Commissioner, or by one of the Commissioners, to sign currency notes, shall be subscribed to every such note, and may be impressed thereon by machinery.

<small>Signatures notes.</small>

(2) Names so impressed shall be taken to be valid signatures.

11. The Head Commissioner, the Commissioners and the Deputy Commissioners shall, in their respective

Issue of notes for silver by Head Commissioner, Commissioners and Deputy Commissioners. Circles of Issue, on the demand of any person, issue, from the office or offices of issue established in their respective circles, currency notes of the denominations prescribed under this Act, in exchange for the amount thereof—

(a) In current silver coin of the Government of India;

(b) [*Repealed by Act VIII. of* 1893];

(c) In current silver coin made under the Native Coinage Act, 1876 (IX. of 1876), as to which coin a declaration has been made under section 3 of that Act ; *or*

(d) [*Repealed by Act VIII. of* 1893.]

Issue of notes for silver by Currency Agents. 12. Any Currency Agent to whom notes have been supplied under section 9 may, if he thinks fit, on the demand of any person, issue from his agency any such notes in exchange for the amount thereof in any coin specified in clause (a) or clause (c) of section 11.

Issue of notes for gold. 13. The Governor-General in Council may, from time to time, by order notified in the *Gazette* of India, direct that currency notes shall be issued at such offices of issue as are named in the order, in exchange for gold coin of full weight of the Government of India, or for foreign gold coin or gold bullion, at the rates, and according to the rules and conditions, fixed by that order.

14. [*Melting and assaying bullion or coin received for notes.*] *Repeal by Act VIII.* of 1893.

15. [*Certificates for bullion or coin.*] *Repeal by Act VIII. of* 1893.

IV. NOTES WHERE LEGAL TENDER AND WHERE PAYABLE.

Notes where legal tender. 16. Within any of the said Circles of Issue, a currency note issued from any town in that circle shall be a legal tender for the amount expressed in that note, in payment or on account of—

    (a) Any revenue or other claim, to the amount of five rupees and upwards, due to the Government of India, and

    (b) Any sum of five rupees and upwards, due by the Government of India, or by any body corporate or person in British India :

Provided that no such note shall be deemed to be a legal tender by the Government of India at any office of issue.

17. A currency note shall be payable only—   Notes where payable.

    (a) At the office or offices of issue of the town from which it has been issued, and

    (b) In the case of notes issued from any town not situate in British Burma, also at the Presidency-town of the Presidency within which that town is situate.

18. For the purposes of sections 16 and 17, notes issued from any Currency Agency shall be deemed to have been issued from the town appointed under section 5 to be the place of issue in the Circle of Issue in which that Agency is established.   Notes issued from Currency Agencies to be deemed to be issued from place of Issue of Circle.

V. RESERVE.

19. The whole amount of the coin and bullion received under this Act, and under Act III. of 1871, for currency notes, shall be retained and secured as a reserve to pay those notes, with the exception of such an amount, not exceeding one hundred millions of rupees, as the Governor-General in Council, with the consent of the Secretary of State for India, from time to time fixes.   Coin and bullion received for notes to be kept as a reserve, except amount fixed as herein provided.

Investment of such amount.

20. The amount so fixed shall be published in the *Gazette* of India, and the whole, or such part thereof as the Governor-General in Council from time to time fixes, shall be invested in securities of the Government of India.

Appropriation of coin, bullion and securities.

21. (1) The said coin, bullion and securities shall be appropriated and set apart to provide for the satisfaction and discharge of the said notes; and the said notes shall be deemed to have been issued on the security of the said coin, bullion and securities, as well as on the general credit of the Government of India:

Provided that any coin or bullion so received and appropriated may be sold or exchanged for gold or silver coin of the Government of India of the like value, which shall be so appropriated and set apart instead of the coin or bullion sold or exchanged.

(2) [*Repealed by Act VIII. of* 1893.]

Trustees of securities purchased under Act.

22. The securities purchased under section 20 shall be held by the Head Commissioner and the Master of the Mint at Calcutta, in trust for the Secretary of State for India in Council.

Power to sell and replace securities.

23. (1) The Head Commissioner may, at any time when ordered so to do by the Governor-General in Council, sell and dispose of any portion of the above-mentioned investment.

(2) For the purpose of effecting such sales, the Master of the Mint at Calcutta shall, on a request in writing from the Head Commissioner, at all times sign and endorse the securities, and the Head Commissioner, if so directed by the Governor-General in Council, may purchase securities of the Government of India to replace such sales.

Accounts of interest on securities.

24. (1) The interest accruing due on the securities purchased and held under this Act shall be entered in a

separate account to be annually rendered by the Head Commissioner to the Governor-General in Council.

(2) The amount of the interest shall, from time to time, as it becomes due, be paid to the credit of the Government of India, under the head of " Profits of Notes Circulation ".

(3) An account, showing the amount of the profits and of the charges and expenses incidental thereto, shall be made up and published annually in the *Gazette* of India.

VI. PRIVATE BILLS PAYABLE TO BEARER ON DEMAND.

25. No body corporate or person in British India shall draw, accept, make or issue any bill of exchange, hundí, promissory note or engagement for the payment of money payable to bearer on demand, or borrow, owe or take up any sum or sums of money on the bills, hundís or notes payable to bearer on demand, of any such body corporate or of any such person :

Prohibition of issue of private bills or notes payable to beare on demand.

Provided that cheques or drafts, payable to bearer on demand or otherwise, may be drawn on bankers, shroffs or agents, by their customers or constituents, in respect of deposits of money in the hands of those bankers, shroffs or agents and held by them at the credit and dis_ posal of the persons drawing such cheques or drafts.

26. (1) Any body corporate or person committing any offence under section 25 shall, on conviction before a Presidency magistrate, or a magistrate of the first class, be punished with a fine equal to the amount of the bill, hundí, note or engagement in respect whereof the offence is committed.

Penalty for issuing such bills or notes

(2) Every prosecution under this section shall be insti- tuted by the Head Commissioner, Commissioner or Deputy Commissioner, as the case may be, of Paper

Prosecutions

Currency for the Circle of Issue in which the bill, hundí, note or engagement is drawn, accepted, made or issued.

VII. MISCELLANEOUS.

Monthly abstracts of accounts.

27. An abstract of the accounts of the Department of Paper Currency, showing—

(a) The whole amount of currency notes in circulation;

(b) The amount of coin and bullion reserved, distinguishing gold from silver; and

(c) The nominal value of, and the price paid for, the Government securities held by the said Department,

Shall be made up monthly by the Head Commissioner, and published, as soon as may be, in the *Gazette* of India.

Supplementary powers of the Government of India.

28. (1) The Governor-General in Council may, from time to time, by notification in the *Gazette* of India—

(a) Fix the amounts (not being less than five rupees) for which currency notes shall be issued ;

(b) Alter the limits of any of the Circles of Issue ;

(c) Declare the places at which currency notes shall be issued ;

(d) Fix the rates, rules and conditions at and according to which gold may be taken in exchange for currency notes ;

(e) Fix the charge for melting and assaying bullion and foreign coin received for such notes ;

(f) [*Repealed by Act VIII. of* 1893] ;

(g) Regulate any matters relative to paper currency which are not provided for by this Act; and

(h) Revoke or alter any notification previously published under this Act.

(2) Every notification under this section shall come into force on the day therein in that behalf mentioned and shall have effect as if it were enacted in this Act

(3) [*Repealed by Act VIII. of* 1893.]

NOTIFICATIONS.

Simla, the 26th June, 1893.

No. 2662. The Governor-General in Council hereby announces that, until further orders, gold coins and gold bullion will be received by the Mint Masters of the Calcutta and Bombay mints respectively in exchange for Government rupees, at the rate of 7·53344 grains troy of fine gold for one rupee, on the following conditions :—

(1) Such coin or bullion must be fit for coinage.

(2) The quantity tendered at one time must not be less than 50 tolas.

(3) A charge of one-fourth per mille will be made on all gold coin or bullion which is melted or cut so as to render the same fit for receipt into the mint.

(4) The Mint Master, on receipt of gold coin or bullion into the mint, shall grant to the proprietor a receipt which shall entitle him to a certificate from the Mint and Assay Masters for the amount of rupees to be given in exchange for such coin or bullion payable at the General (Reserve) Treasury, Calcutta or Bombay. Such certificates shall be payable at the General Treasury after such lapse of time from the issue thereof as the Comptroller-General may fix from time to time.

No. 2663. In supersession of the notification by the Government of India in the Financial Department, No. 3287, dated the 28th October, 1868, which is hereby cancelled, the Governor-General in Council is pleased to direct that, from and after the date of this notification, sovereigns and half-sovereigns of current weight coined at

any authorised royal mint in England or Australia shall
be received in all the treasuries of British India and its
dependencies, in payment of sums due to the Government,
as the equivalent of fifteen rupees and of seven rupees and
eight annas, respectively.

No. 2664. In exercise of the powers conferred by the
Indian Paper Currency Act, 1882, as amended by the
Indian Coinage and Paper Currency Act, 1893, and of all
other powers enabling him in this behalf, the Governor-
General in Council is pleased to direct that currency notes
shall be issued by the Head Commissioner of Paper
Currency, Calcutta, and by the Commissioner of Paper
Currency, Bombay, on the requisition of the Comptroller-
General, in exchange for gold coin or gold bullion, at the
rate of one Government rupee for 7·53344 grains troy
of fine gold. Sovereigns and half-sovereigns of current
weight coined at any authorised royal mint in England or
Australia shall be taken as the equivalent of fifteen rupees
and of seven rupees and eight annas, respectively.

Note.—Under a notification issued on September 10,
1897, the reserve treasuries at Calcutta, Madras and
Bombay are also authorised to receive sovereigns and
half-sovereigns at the rate of fifteen rupees per sovereign.

INDIAN CURRENCY.

(Reprinted from the *Bankers' Magazine* for April, 1896.)

In December, 1892, I read a paper before the Institute of Bankers advocating the closure of the Indian mints to the coinage of silver, the receipt of gold at the rate of 1s. 3d. for the rupee, and the retention of such gold in the paper currency reserve, in view to the establishment of the rupee on a permanent gold basis at that rate. In June, 1893, the Indian mints were closed for the public coinage of silver by law. But though the receipt of gold at the rate of 1s. 4d. for the rupee, and its retention in the paper currency reserve at that rate, were authorised by notification, these measures were not given the force of law. Neither was any restriction put on the power of the State to coin silver on its own account.

The following bill was originally drafted, shortly after the paper was read, to put into a definite shape the plan I proposed. It has since been modified, corrected and improved. The rate of 1s. 4d. (adopted as the temporary rate by the Government) has been taken instead of 1s. 3d., the rate which I originally proposed; for though no doubt the lower rate has been proved to have been the best, there is much to be said in favour of the higher rate. It is hoped that the publication of the bill in this form may lead to the proposal receiving careful consideration.

8

DRAFT BILL

To further amend the Indian Coinage and Paper Currency
Acts (XXIII. of 1870 and XX. of 1882).

Preamble.. WHEREAS it is expedient to provide so that the rupee currency of British India may hereafter be based on
gold : It is hereby enacted as follows :—

Short title. 1. This Act may be called " The Indian Gold Standard Act ".

Local extent. It extends to the whole of British India ;

Commence-
ment. And it shall come into force on the passing thereof.

Acts partly
repealed. 2. The enactments specified in the Schedule hereto
annexed shall be repealed or modified to the extent and in
the manner mentioned in the third column thereof, but
no such repeal or modification shall affect anything
already done or any right or modification heretofore
acquired or undergone under the said enactments or any
of them.

Standard
gold. 3. Wherever standard gold is referred to in this Act or
in Act XX. of 1882, it shall mean metal containing eleven
parts of fine gold, and one part of alloy.

Established
gold par. 4. The rate of 123·27447 grains troy of standard gold
for fifteen rupees shall be, and shall be called, the established gold par.

Standard
gold bars. 5. Gold received under clause (e) of section 11 of Act
XX. of 1882 may, and all gold received under clauses (f)
and (g) of that section shall, be made into bars of standard gold of such weight as the Governor-General in
Council may from time to time prescribe, but such gold
bars shall not weigh less than 8218·3 grains troy (representing one thousand rupees) each.

Gold notes. 6. Currency notes of ten thousand rupees issued after
the passing of this Act shall be called gold notes, and, not-

withstanding anything in Act XX. of 1882, or in notifications issued under that Act, shall not be issued in exchange for coins received under clauses (a) and (c), but only in exchange for coins and bullion received under clauses (e), (f) and (g) of section 11 of Act XX. of 1882 ; and shall be promissory notes payable at the option of the holder, either in current silver coin of the Government of India or in gold. If payment of a gold note shall be required in gold, payment shall be made, at the option of the Head Commissioner, Commissioners, or Deputy Commissioners of Currency as the case may be, either by £666 10s. in full legal tender British gold coin, and two rupees and one half-rupee, or by standard gold bars weighing 82,183 grains troy.

Currency notes of denominations less than ten thousand rupees, the issue of which may be prescribed under Act XX. of 1882, shall be called rupee notes, and shall be issued in exchange for coin or bullion received under clauses (a), (c), (e), (f) and (g) of section 11 of that Act ; and shall be payable in current silver coin of the Government of India. Rupee notes only shall be issued under section 12 of Act XX. of 1882.

Rupee notes.

7. The Head Commissioner, Commissioners and Deputy Commissioners may require any bullion or coins received under section 11, clause (g) of Act XX. of 1882 to be melted and assayed.

Expense of melting and assaying bullion received for notes.

Any loss of weight caused by such melting or assay shall be borne by the person tendering the bullion or coin.

8. Every person so tendering bullion or coins under section 11, clause (g) of Act XX. of 1882, shall, after the expiration of the time necessary for melting and assaying the same, be entitled to receive therefor a certificate signed by the person authorised to issue the notes aforesaid.

Certificates for bullion.

Contents of
certificate.

Such certificate shall—

(a) Acknowledge the receipt of such bullion or coin ;

(b) State the amount of notes issued under this Act, or of such notes and cash to which the holder is entitled in exchange for such bullion or coins ;

(c) State the interval, which shall be fixed from time to time by the Comptroller-General, but which shall not be more than fifteen days, on the expiration of which, if the certificate be presented to such office, the holder shall be entitled to receive such notes and cash.

Gold note
reserve.

9. The whole amount of gold coin and bullion received in exchange for gold notes as prescribed by section 6 of this Act, or the standard gold bars into which it may be made under section 5, shall, until (as hereinafter prescribed) the Governor-General in Council shall have notified that the Currency Department will at all times give gold at the established gold par in exchange for rupees and rupee notes if brought for the purpose in quantities of ten thousand rupees, be appropriated and set apart as a special reserve to pay such notes so long as they are outstanding ; such reserve shall be called the gold note reserve, and such notes shall be deemed to have been issued on the general credit of the Government, as well as on the security of the gold note reserve.

General
metallic
reserve.

10. The remainder of the coin and bullion received under Act XX. of 1882 shall be called the general metallic reserve, and shall be set aside and secured, except as hereinafter provided, for the payment of rupee notes. If any gold notes are tendered in exchange for silver coins, such silver coins shall be taken from the general metallic reserve and a corresponding amount of

gold at the established gold par shall be transferred from
the gold note reserve to, and shall form part of, the
general metallic reserve.

11. The Secretary of State for India shall from time Investment
to time fix the amount of the general metallic reserve general of portion of
which may be invested ; but such amount shall not exceed metallic
half the average amount of rupee notes in circulation reserve.
during the previous three years ; and it shall not exceed
one hundred millions * of rupees, until, as hereinafter
prescribed, the Governor-General in Council shall have
notified that the Currency Department will at all times
give gold at the established gold par, in exchange for
rupees and rupee notes, if brought for the purpose in
quantities of ten thousand rupees.

12. The amount so fixed shall be published in the Description
Gazette of India, and the whole or such part thereof as of invest- ment.
the Governor-General in Council from time to time fixes
shall be invested in securities of the Government of India,
or in gold securities guaranteed by the British Government. Any investment above one hundred millions of
rupees shall be in gold securities guaranteed by the
British Government.

13. The said general metallic reserves and the said Appropria-
securities shall be appropriated and set apart to provide general tion of.
for the satisfaction and discharge of the said rupee notes, metallic reserve and
and the said rupee notes shall be deemed to have been securities.
issued on the security of such general metallic reserve
and such securities as well as on the general credit of the
Government.

14. Whenever the silver in the general metallic reserve Coinage of
constitutes less than one-half of the total of such general silver.
metallic reserve, the Governor-General in Council may

* [Altered from eighty to one hundred millions in consequence of the
alteration of the law in 1896.]

order the Mint Master to coin, under Act XXIII. of 1870, for such general metallic reserve, rupees, half-rupees, quarter-rupees and eighth of rupees ; and may either issue notes in payment for such silver at its bullion value, or pay for it at its bullion value either in gold or silver from the general metallic reserve ; but only so much shall be coined as shall bring the proportion of the general metallic reserve held in silver up to one-half of the whole.

Equivalence Fund.   The excess value of the coins coined over the bullion value shall be taken in gold at the established par from the general metallic reserve, and shall be set aside as an Equivalence Fund, apart from the general metallic reserve, for the purpose of securing the difference between the bullion value of the silver coins and their nominal gold value.

Further coinage of silver.   15. No coinage of silver other than that provided for under section 14 of this Act shall be authorised except in exchange for a corresponding weight of silver coins, coined under Acts XVII. of 1835, XXI. of 1838, XIII. of 1862, and XXIII. of 1870, or under this Act.

Additions to Equivalence Fund.   16. It shall be lawful for the Government of India from time to time, as it may think fit, to use any part of the revenues of India for the purchase of gold to be added to the Equivalence Fund. Any such addition to the Equivalence Fund shall be only available for the purposes of the fund as laid down in this Act.

Exchange of silver and silver notes into gold.   17. At any time after the portion of the general metallic reserve held in silver has continuously for one year been less than that held in gold, the Governor-General in Council may, by notification published in the *Gazette* of India, declare that, on and after some specified date, but not earlier than three months from the date of the notification, the Head Commissioner, Commissioners, and Deputy Commissioners of Currency shall at all times give gold at the established gold par, in exchange for rupees or for rupee notes, if presented for the purpose in quantities of ten thousand rupees, and the silver coin so received shall take the place of the gold in the general metallic reserve ; and thereafter the officers above named shall always be bound to give gold at the established gold par in exchange for rupees or rupee notes if presented in quantities of ten thousand rupees.

18. On the issue of the notification prescribed by section 17 of this Act, transfers to the Equivalence Fund under sections 14 and 16 shall cease, and the gold then in the Equivalence Fund and the gold in the gold note reserve shall be transferred to, and form part of, the general metallic reserve. And all the gold in this general metallic reserve shall be available for securing the exchange into gold of gold notes, rupees and rupee notes, without priority of either over the other, and the gold notes and the rupee notes shall be deemed to have been issued on, and the rupees in circulation shall be deemed to be supported by, the security of such general metallic reserve, and of the invested securities, as well as by the general credit of the Government of India. *Absorption of Equivalence Fund and gold note reserve, and application of general metallic reserve.*

19. In addition to the information, the publication of which is required by section 27 of Act XX. of 1882, the abstract of the accounts of the Department of Issue shall show separately :— *Monthly abstracts of accounts.*

(a) The gold notes in circulation.

(b) The rupee notes in circulation.

(c) The gold reserved for gold notes.

(d) The gold reserved for rupee notes.

(e) The gold for the Equivalence Fund.

(f) The securities of the Government of India.

(g) The securities guaranteed by the British Government.

(h) The rates at which gold coins shall be received under clause (f), section 11 of Act II. of 1882.

THE SCHEDULE OF ENACTMENTS REPEALED OR MODIFIED REFERRED TO
IN SECTION 2.

Number, Year and Short Title of Act.	Sections.	Extent of Repeal or Modification.
Act XXIII. of 1870. The Indian Coin-age Act, 1870.	Sections 4 and 5.	Both sections repealed.
Act XX. of 1882. The Indian Paper Currency Act, 1882.	Section 8.	The words "ten thousand rupees and such smaller sums" to be substituted for "such sums".
	Section 11.	The following clauses and proviso to be added :— (e) In full legal tender gold coins of the United Kingdom at the rate of fifteen rupees for £1. (f) In gold coins other than full legal tender coins of the United Kingdom, at such rates as the Governor-General in Council may from time to time by notification in the *Gazette* of India prescribe, or (g) In gold bullion or gold coins (on condition of such bullion and coins being fit for coinage) in quantities of fifty tolas and upwards, at the rate of fifteen rupees for 123·27447 grains of standard gold. Provided that the amounts so calculated, so far as they represent fractions of the smallest note issuable under this Act, may be paid in cash.
	Section 12.	The following words and letters " or clause (e) or clause (f)" to be added after the words " or clause (c)".
	Sections 13, 19, 20, 21.	The whole to be repealed.
	Section 22.	The words "this Act or any Act by which it may be amended" to be substituted for the words " Section 20 ".
	Section 23.	The words " or securities guaranteed by the British Government" to be inserted after the words "Government of India" in clause (2).
	Section 24.	The words " or any Act by which it may be amended" to be inserted after the words " this Act " in clause (1).
	Section 28.	Clause (d) to be repealed.

STATEMENT OF OBJECTS AND REASONS.

This bill is intended to provide for the silver currency of India being secured on a gold basis when the gold value of the rupee reaches 1s. 4d.

It is based on the knowledge that, if the State paper currency can be secured on a gold basis, this, *ipso facto*, places the silver rupee currency on the same basis.

It recognises the determination of the Government to make the silver rupee an efficient representative of 8·2183 grains troy of British standard gold, that is to say of 1s. 4d.

It gives the force of law and permanence to the notification under which gold can be received at the Indian treasuries at that rate, and provides that gold so received shall be part of the paper currency reserve, being held in the form of either full legal tender gold coins of the United Kingdom, or gold bars representing not less than Rs. 1000 each. It provides for the retention of such gold in the paper currency reserve until either it is required to purchase silver when the coinage of silver rupees is proved to be necessary, or the State finds itself in a position to undertake to redeem its notes in gold bullion when presented in quantities of not less than Rs. 10,000.

It repeals the existing law (sections 4 and 5, Act XXIII. of 1870) under which gold may be coined at the Indian mints, and makes no provision for a gold currency.

It takes away the power which the Government now has of coining rupees at its discretion, placing an automatic limit, dependent on the relative amounts of gold and silver in the paper currency reserve, on the further coinage of rupees.

It provides that, in the event of such further coinage,

the difference between the nominal and intrinsic gold values of the coins shall be set apart in gold as a reserve, and it permits the Government to add to the gold reserve from the general revenues of India.

It restricts the future issue of notes convertible into rupees to denominations of less than Rs. 10,000.

It provides for the issue of special gold notes of Rs. 10,000 in exchange for, and convertible into, gold, so that before the currency is placed on an effective gold basis it may be possible to withdraw without loss gold which may have been sent to India when the par was reached, and which it may subsequently, owing to a fall in exchange, be desirable to withdraw.

It empowers (though it does not require) the Government, so soon as certain conditions as to the relative amounts of gold and silver in the paper currency reserve have been arrived at, to permanently place the currency of the country on a gold basis by undertaking to give gold bullion in exchange for rupees or rupee notes if presented for the purpose in quantities of Rs. 10,000.

It provides that, after the Government has undertaken this responsibility, the Secretary of State may increase the security investment of the Paper Currency Department above the present limit of one hundred millions of rupees up to one-half of the average rupee notes in circulation during the three preceding years, all excess over the present limit being in gold securities guaranteed by the British Government.

INDEX.

ABERDEEN UNIVERSITY PRESS.

www.ingramcontent.com/pod-product-compliance
Lightning Source LLC
Chambersburg PA
CBHW030607270326
41927CB00007B/1082